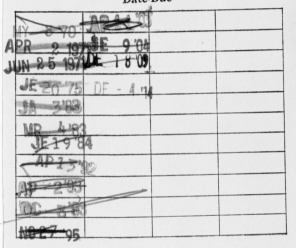

LOS ANGELES: A PROFILE

LOS ANGELES

A Profile

BY W. W. ROBINSON

UNIVERSITY OF OKLAHOMA PRESS : NORMAN

The Forest and the People (1946)

Land in California (1948)

The Indians of Los Angeles (1952)

Panorama: *A Picture History of Southern California* (1953)

The Malibu (with Lawrence Clark Powell) (1958)

Lawyers of Los Angeles (1959)

Los Angeles from the Days of the Pueblo (1959)

The Story of the Southwest Museum (1960)

People Versus Lugo (1962)

The Key to Los Angeles (1963)

Little History of a Big City (miniature) (1963)

Zamorano Choice (compiled, edited) (1966)

Maps of Los Angeles (1966)

Los Angeles: *A Profile* (1968)

The paper on which this book is printed bears the watermark of the University of Oklahoma Press and is designed for an effective life of at least three hundred years.

Library of Congress Catalog Card Number: 68–15675

Copyright 1968 by the University of Oklahoma Press, Publishing Division of the University. Composed and printed at Norman, Oklahoma, U.S.A., by the University of Oklahoma Press. First edition.

To My Favorite Angeleno: Irene Robinson

CONTENTS

1.	Front-Page City	*page* 3
2.	Why Is There a Los Angeles?	9
3.	The Profile of Los Angeles	18
4.	Motorized City	27
5.	Hollywood Impact	35
6.	Minority Report	44
7.	Cultural "Detonation"	55
8.	Spanish-Mexican Heritage	73
9.	Expanding Empire of a Newspaper	85
10.	Myth-Making	98
11.	Vital City	112
	Books About Los Angeles	125
	Index	133
	Map of Los Angeles Area	20–21

LOS ANGELES: A PROFILE

1

Front-Page City

PERHAPS NO CITY in the United States has inspired as much pungent comment from visitors as Los Angeles. A quarter of a century ago I gathered together a selection of remarks made by visitors to this city. The verbal tidbits chosen were largely acrid, hostile, corrosive, belittling, scornful, sometimes wise and illuminating, almost always amusing. The collection resulted in an anthology of lively reading published under the title *What They Say About the Angels*. The collector—I was the collector—was described on the dust jacket as pouncing "upon a new insult as avidly as a butterfly-chaser brings down his net over a new species of Lepidoptera."

The background picture of Los Angeles, presented chronologically in the collection—from the time of the birth of the eleven-family Spanish pueblo—was that of a city taking shape.

Los Angeles is still taking shape and is still drawing comment. However, the comments are changing in character. The reasons behind these changes help to justify calling the city a "center of civilization."

Los Angeles has rather enjoyed the quips it has inspired.

Such shrewd pleasantries as "Sea-Coast of Iowa," "Attica minus the Intellect," "six suburbs in search of a city," "the Great American Commonplace," "the Kook Capital of the World," "Moronia," "so incredibly ordinary," and "a body without a navel" are the creations of distinguished literary figures. This type of comment was well under way by 1842 when Sir George Simpson of the Hudson's Bay Company, in his journey around the world, described the tiny pueblo of Los Angeles as being "the noted abode of the lowest drunkards and gamblers of the country." During the following century and a quarter, commentators have often competed in the virulence of their descriptive remarks. My personal favorite is a Lucius Beebe gem: "Everytime I find myself in Los Angeles I wonder what I've done to displease God."

The alleged war between Los Angeles and San Francisco —begetting occasional naughty outbursts from both towns —has been mostly a publicity stunt. The average Angeleno never heard of the battle, in spite of the frequent attempts by the Los Angeles *Times* and the San Francisco *Chronicle* to stir up bellicosity by sending their sharpest columnists north and south to spy upon the other city. *The Saturday Evening Post* at one time matched Herb Caen of San Francisco against Jack Smith of Los Angeles. Caen placed the origins of his city's hatred of Los Angeles with the boom of the twenties, when the population of the southern city shot ahead while the population of San Francisco stood still. Smith, on the other hand, attempted to show why San Franciscans really hated Angelenos. He said the northerners looked narcissistically into their magic mirrors, were blind to the creeping decay behind the pretty skyline, and feared that the Angelenos' "despised culture of hot-dog architecture, crackpot faiths, toreador pants, graveyard art and automobile worship might flow north and corrupt them." Defender Caen ended his argument with his favorite bon mot: "Isn't it nice that the kind of people who prefer Los Angeles to San Francisco live there?" A few other skirmishes took place during the middle 1960's with the publicity caused by Los Angeles' so-called "cultural explosion." Paul Coates of Los Angeles was dispatched to San Francisco. He reported back that "knocking L.A. was a holy crusade." Stan Delaplane of San Francisco called on Los Angeles and found a "city zeroed in on culture."

Los Angeles in recent years, because of its geographical spread, its freeway system, and its particular problems, has drawn a new kind of comment. The magazine *Fortune* described Los Angeles as the "prototype of the super-city," while the *New Yorker* labeled it the "ultimate city." Los Angeles and all of Southern California were called a "preview of things to come" by Richard G. Lillard in his *Eden in Jeopardy*. "What happens in Southern California happens elsewhere sooner or later," wrote Richard Elman in *Ill-At-Ease in Compton*. For his students, George Dudley, dean of the School of Architecture and Urban Planning in the University of California at Los Angeles, found the sprawling city "a living laboratory." These descriptions of an expanding, explosive area are partly complimentary; they can also serve as warnings to urban dwellers. In and around Los Angeles, man has meddled with his environment—he has polluted the air, the sea, and the scenery, and he has attempted to destroy agriculture. But he has also solved many problems in what the local citizenry believes to be America's most mobile, stimulating, and exciting area.

The phrase "Los Angeles area" is used extensively in this book, for the actual municipal boundaries of Los Angeles are as nondescript as a splash of ink and are of interest only

5

to City Hall. Angelenos, cruising about in their automobiles, know nothing about them. It will help to think of the old downtown district, much enlarged, as "Central City." That is the present term for that core which the city has always had, though in smaller form. The essential boundaries of this core are the Harbor Freeway on the west, Alameda Street on the east, the Hollywood–San Bernardino Freeway on the north, and the Santa Monica Freeway on the south. Central City is the heart of the municipal area. It is surrounded by the many satellite communities and cities of at least Los Angeles County. Parts of Orange and Ventura counties should be swept into the embracing phrase—the Los Angeles area. However, the boundaries of the satellites have little significance either. These individual enclaves, whether incorporated or not, are like the present-day burroughs of metropolitan London which originated in villages and suburbs outside the old city. The official administrative bodies have exchange agreements, usually with the city or the county of Los Angeles, covering fire and police protection and other necessary services.

What physically exists throughout the Los Angeles area is an increasingly close-knit kind of city-state, surrounded and crossed by an intricate system of freeways. This closely-knit area will call ultimately for regional government. The freeways are the "sinews of the supercity," to use the apt phrase of Larry Meyer, editor of *Westways*, the monthly magazine of the Automobile Club of Southern California. The sinews link and draw together all the parts of the Los Angeles area, including the proud little municipality of Beverly Hills, which is surrounded entirely by the city of Los Angeles, and such imaginative communities as Century City and Bel-Air, which are specialized developments within the corporate limits of Los Angeles.

"Southern California," another frequently used phrase, is another area difficult to define. The Security First National Bank, with headquarters in Los Angeles, puts out an important, monthly business summary, much sought after by businessmen and newsmen. This publication tries to use "Southland," but very often uses "Southern California" when referring to California's fourteen southernmost counties. These fourteen counties largely recognize Los Angeles as their financial center. Fresno County, the most northerly of the fourteen, has some differences of opinion—some qualms—about being classed with Southern California. Some of its citizens are northern in feeling and refer to San Francisco as "The City." The coastal counties south of Monterey County are unquestionably "southern" now, as they were during the cattle-raising, rancho days of the preceding Mexican and Spanish periods. But if one could determine exactly where the dominance of Los Angeles ends and that of San Francisco begins, that meeting place would be the dividing line between Southern and Northern California. Since spheres of dominance overlap, however, there will continue to be argument.

The old phrase "South of the Tehachapis" has no meaning now in defining Southern California. It lost its significance and became outmoded when freeways and airways destroyed the barrier of the Tehachapi Mountains. That barrier formerly made the area to the south a kind of island surrounded by mountains on the north, the Pacific Ocean on the west, the desert on the east, and Mexico on the south.

As a center of civilization, and even as a center of culture, Los Angeles has been of some importance ever since its beginning days. The old pueblo was in the heart of Southern California's ranchos—a social, trading, and business center for the Spanish-speaking people whose livelihood depended

7

on the raising of long-horned cattle. Later the gospel of sunshine, perpetual health, and easy living, preached during the real estate boom of the 1880's, affected the nation. The boom of the 1920's caused a wholesale migration of people to Southern California by automobile. This migration effected a transformation in the way of living for the newcomers and for all Angelenos, and even influenced eastern non-migrants. The rise of Hollywood had a massive impact on the manners, morals, and thinking of the whole world. The continuing activities of Los Angeles in creating, facing, or solving fundamental urban problems have been and are of nationwide significance. All of these factors have made Los Angeles a center of civilization.

2

Why Is There a Los Angeles?

THE QUESTION, "Why is there a Los Angeles?" arises in the minds of many non-Angelenos, especially of those who are confounded by the city's expansive growth in a semi-desert, water-poor area.

"It is difficult to find any real good reason why the city of Los Angeles should have come into existence," wrote Raymond Dasmann, chairman of the Division of Natural Resources in Humboldt State College in Northern California. His statement appears in his *The Destruction of California* (1965).

A look at a geographic map of California and at the migratory movements of people from earliest days will supply a quick answer to the question. Since prehistoric times, human beings have been pouring into the Los Angeles basin and making it continuously a widely populated region. Migrants arrived seeking a better climate and an easier life. They went there primarily because the natural gateways and approaches from the north, east, and southeast inevitably led them into the valleys, plains, and rolling hills that are now contained in the metropolitan area of Los Angeles. The Owens Valley access from the north, the

Cajon Pass entrance from the east, and the San Gorgonio Pass leading in from the southeast determined the destination of the processions of brown-skinned people who sought to better themselves.

At least fifteen hundred years ago, Shoshonean-speaking Indians began streaming into Southern California, legendarily by way of Cajon Pass in what is now San Bernardino County. They or their ancestors had come down from Owens Valley, ultimately from Nevada and other northeastern areas. Probably they gradually drove a wedge through the Hokan-speaking Indian inhabitants, of whose settling of the area little is known. The Shoshonean-speaking Indians established brush-hut villages that dotted the landscape over what is now Los Angeles and Orange counties and settled on offshore islands such as Santa Catalina. At that time there were year-round streams—the Los Angeles, the San Gabriel, and the Santa Ana rivers, along with various creeks—which all emptied into the Pacific Ocean. Native oak trees furnished acorns, an all-season, staple food. The chaparral on the hillsides provided an unlimited source of food, drink, medicine, and even weapons. Small game supplied meat and, when needed, clothing. The seashore villagers were shellfish-eaters and deep-sea fishermen, driving their pine-plank canoes out through the Pacific waters. Little clothing was required in the mild climate.

Next came the Spaniards, Mexicans, and Anglo-Americans, either by ship or overland from Mexico. Los Angeles, which had been started in 1781 as a Spanish pueblo, became California's most populous town during the cattle-raising era of the Spanish-speaking *rancheros*.

Pioneer Jedediah Smith, carrying a Bible and a gun and accompanied by his band of trappers, reached San Gabriel Mission and Los Angeles in the fall of 1826, finding entrance into Southern California through Cajon Pass. They had crossed the San Bernardino County area from the Colorado River and the east—the first men from United States territory to make the overland trip into California. Other trapping parties followed. Their pioneering treks led to the development and establishment of Santa Fe–Los Angeles pack-train caravans, following what became known as the Old Spanish Trail. Traders, using this approach to the pueblo of Los Angeles, brought blankets and manufactured goods from New Mexico to be exchanged for horses and mules in California. Some of the newcomers became settlers, married *Californio* daughters, and played leading roles as merchants and *rancheros*.

Trappers, traders, and settlers, approaching Southern California through the historic gateways used by their Indian predecessors, traveled first by horseback, later by wagon and railroad, and ultimately by automobile. They arrived unavoidably, or inevitably, in the pueblo, later the city, of Los Angeles.

Railroads found access to Los Angeles and Southern California from the north through the San Joaquin Valley, later from the east through the Cajon and San Gorgonio passes, essentially following old pathways. The Southern Pacific was the pioneer in the middle 1870's. When the very competitive Santa Fe Railway made its appearance in Los Angeles in the 1880's, via Cajon Pass, a rate war began which resulted in bringing thousands of newcomers into Southern California and ushering in a real estate boom which climaxed in 1888. A third railroad, built in 1905, became ultimately a part of the Union Pacific System. It also made use of Cajon Pass.

So, too, automobiles, using the first cross-country highways created for them and arriving in Los Angeles by way

11

of the prehistoric paths, started the great boom of the twenties. The influx in the early 1920's of people, mostly young people, was almost a mass migration of Anglo-Americans to Los Angeles.

Los Angeles had begun in the 1700's as a carefully planned farming village, its site chosen for the "fertility of the soil" and the "abundance of water for irrigation." *El Pueblo de Nuestra Señora de Los Angeles de Porciúncula* became Los Angeles in 1850, after California had been taken, by conquest, into the United States. It was and continued to be the magnet for migrants seeking easy living and a mild climate in the Southwest.

At first the Angelenos and their predecessors had plenty of water. The Indians relied on rivers, creeks, and springs. The same water sources took care of pueblo townsmen and those living on the surrounding ranchos. By the 1870's, however, the landscape of the Los Angeles area was dotted with windmills, flowing wells, flumes, and, in the town, open canals or *zanjas* carrying river water. Underground sources were being drawn upon to supplement the water from the rivers.

Even through the great boom of the eighties, Angelenos and those living outside the city boundaries seemed to have enough water for a vast planting of citrus and other agricultural crops and for city expansion and the laying out of new towns. By 1900, rivers were inadequate, and the underground water levels were dropping. Artesian wells had to be drilled ever deeper. Angelenos were beginning to fear a waterless future.

Los Angeles became aqueduct-minded and took dramatic action. The city built the Los Angeles-Owens Valley Aqueduct, a major engineering feat and a triumph for engineer William Mulholland, for it crossed rugged mountains and sun-baked deserts. Mountain water began flowing into the Los Angeles area on November 5, 1913. Because of a developing feud between the Owens Valley people and Angelenos, featuring dynamiting episodes, Los Angeles ultimately bought nearly the entire valley, including its five towns. Then the Mono Basin watershed was added, making the aqueduct 338 miles long. (Currently a second barrel of the Owens Valley Aqueduct is being completed which will import an additional 150,000 feet of water annually.)

Thirsty Los Angeles kept growing. Because the city realized it would need more water in another twenty-five years, Los Angeles took the lead when a group of Southern California cities organized the Metropolitan Water District of Southern California and constructed Hoover Dam in the Colorado River's Black Canyon. Another giant aqueduct was built across the desert to carry water from the new Lake Mead. The first Colorado River water was delivered to the Los Angeles area on June 17, 1941. A billion gallons a day flowed to the cities that were members of the district.

The next step, for those concerned with water needs in the distant future, has been taken under the leadership of the State of California. Construction on the Feather River Project has begun, with the intention of bringing water from the Northern California streams to be used in many needy areas. A 444-mile aqueduct is called for with the water to be pump-lifted two thousand feet over the Tehachapi Mountains. A branch aqueduct, reaching to Los Angeles and its metropolitan district, will bring water to Castaic Reservoir near San Fernando Valley in 1971 and, in 1972, to Perris Reservoir near Riverside. The metropolitan district will receive the largest single delivery and will pay 70

13

per cent of the cost of the project. Additional water, when needed, can be fed into the Feather River Project's system from California's northern coast.

Los Angeles and Southern California look beyond the year 1990, eyeing still more northerly sources of water, and they are now participating in the completion, on a man-made offshore island, of a great nuclear-fueled plant—the world's largest—to convert seawater into fresh water.

California, Arizona, and the other five Colorado River Basin states, recognizing the inadequacy of the Colorado River, work partly in harmony, partly in conflict, toward obtaining mutually needed waters. The decade-long legal battle over Colorado River water between California and Arizona ended in 1963 when the United States Supreme Court handed down a decree partly adverse to California. Furthermore, the Supreme Court left undecided the basic issue of what to do when there were shortages in the main stream of the river.

Today three million Angelenos—over seven million Angelenos if the Los Angeles County area is being referred to—turn on faucets, and all the water they want or need comes streaming out for drinking, bathing, cooking, washing, irrigating, and filling the thousands of swimming pools that gleam like jewels in the sun. Angelenos give little thought to the sources of this abundance.

Plentiful water made it possible for Los Angeles to expand mightily. For the city to become the focal point of the Southwest, however, a deep-water harbor was needed. In 1890, when Los Angeles had fifty thousand people, the city started a seven-year battle with the powerful Southern Pacific Railroad to have San Pedro, instead of Santa Monica, named by the federal government as the site for such a harbor. California's Senator Stephen M. White, nicknamed "the Little Giant," led and won the fight. A statue of the short, stooped, frock-coated figure of White stands today in front of the Los Angeles County Courthouse, but few Angelenos know who the gentleman was.

Senator White, who had had a spectacular career in law, battled Collis P. Huntington, head of the Southern Pacific Company. The battle lasted until 1899 and was followed closely by Angelenos and by the nation.

In 1891, a board of engineers submitted to Congress a report favoring San Pedro as the site of a deep-water harbor. But the Southern Pacific decided to abandon San Pedro and began work on a long wharf two miles north of Santa Monica which it called the "Port of Los Angeles." A second board of engineers was named, and its report also favored San Pedro. The Los Angeles Chamber of Commerce and the Los Angeles *Times* came out for San Pedro and a "free harbor." While the *Times* did not like "the color of his politics," Senator White, a free-silver Democrat, received complete backing from the newspaper because he favored San Pedro. White, incidentally, was almost as famous for his drinking as for his abilities as a debater. Commentators Alfred Cohn and Joe Chisholm, in *Take the Witness*, said that "when slightly energized by whiskey, his [White's] fine brain functioned with machine-like precision."

When an engineer of national prominence, an employee of "Uncle Collis" P. Huntington, declared Santa Monica superior to San Pedro, the Rivers and Harbors Bill came out of committee with a recommendation of nearly $3,000,000 for a Santa Monica harbor. Senator White then proposed an appropriation for either Santa Monica or San Pedro, as might be determined by a third board of engineers. White talked for three days, largely in debate with Senator Frye of Maine, who suggested that if Los Angeles wanted a harbor

15

it should move to San Diego. White's proposal was adopted, and the new board, in 1897, declared for San Pedro.

Los Angeles celebrated mightily and the siren whistle of the Los Angeles *Times* sounded joyously. Nevertheless, Secretary of War Alger did not set in motion the improvement work. "Uncle Collis" was said to be back of the delay. Finally pressure was brought on President McKinley, through a letter from General William S. Rosecrans, who lived in Los Angeles—he was McKinley's commander during the Civil War. McKinley ordered Alger to ask for bids at once. Alger obeyed, but there was additional delay during the consideration of the bids. After two years of scandalous obstruction, work on the harbor was actually begun in April, 1899. On April 26–27, a great celebration was held in San Pedro, and on the day following, the first load of quarried rock was dumped on the site of the breakwater.

Los Angeles, located twenty miles from the mud flats of San Pedro, had won a great battle. The city proceeded to annex a narrow strip of land connecting Los Angeles with Wilmington, which had ocean frontage. In 1909 the towns of Wilmington and San Pedro consolidated with Los Angeles. Presently, Los Angeles received title to the adjoining tide lands and submerged lands from the state of California. Los Angeles, with federal help, was ready to create the Port of Los Angeles out of the shallow waters, sandbars, and narrow sloughs.

Three transcontinental railroads, converging in San Pedro, along with several hundred trucking firms, have made possible the flow of goods upon the wharves. Since 1923 the tonnage of the water-borne commerce of the Port of Los Angeles has exceeded that of any other port on the Pacific Coast. Behind the port is the huge population of Southern California and the Southwest, making it a gateway

16

to the markets of the world, including the new markets of the Orient.

The cries of seagulls are the background rhythm to this watery gateway. It is redolent with the smell of fish canneries, salt air, harbor water, oil, and new-cut lumber. Huge tankships bring oil from the Persian Gulf, while smaller vessels unload bananas from Central America, molasses from Mexico, automobiles from Europe, steel products from Japan, coffee from Brazil, and copra from the Philippines. Outgoing ships carry steel scraps and cotton for Japan, citrus fruits for France, machinery for Venezuela, and industrial chemicals for the world.

Adjoining the Port of Los Angeles is the Port of Long Beach, for Long Beach started its own harbor project in 1923. Tideland oil revenues have been especially helpful in financing harbor development in the area. There is talk of merging these two competing ports, or at least of consolidating the two port facilities under a joint powers' agreement.

The inevitable use of natural gateways brought Los Angeles into being. Through those gateways people were practically propelled into the Los Angeles basin. Now airplane travel has developed. Twenty million passengers used Los Angeles International Airport in 1967; the redevelopment of the existing airport is being planned, and regional airports are being organized to take care of the needs of the jet age. Now airways are serving as supplements to the historic gateways that made the development of an expanding city possible.

3

The Profile of Los Angeles

IT IS EASY to look at the towering skyline of New York or to observe San Francisco sitting contentedly on her hills and receive single, immediate impressions of these cities, impressions with which everyone will agree.

On the other hand, until the development of the freeways, Los Angeles was hard to look at—literally—by anyone traveling through its interminable maze. Los Angeles did not come easily into focus. Its profile was so illusive that in 1930 one magazine writer glanced at what he could see of the city's 450-square-mile sprawl and remarked, "There is no Los Angeles face!"

With the advent of freeways—the first, the Arroyo Seco Parkway, was dedicated on December 30, 1940—the face of Los Angeles began to show clarity and sharpness of outline. Taking mighty strides through Los Angeles and Orange counties, often called the metropolitan area, the high-flung freeway system reveals, smog permitting, the Los Angeles profile. The physical and architectural outlines become apparent; so, too, the region's drabness and, at the same time, beauty. Dark, towering palms are silhouetted against the sky; massive subdivisions engulf the open fields, former orchards, and chaparral-clad slopes; a Hollywood that for the first time seems fabulous, is revealed; and there is a perpetual backdrop of mountains. With immense

18

curves, the eight-lane highways sweep uninterruptedly through the valleys and hillsides of the Los Angeles basin, now rising just above the tops of red-roofed homes, shopping centers, and industrial complexes; now dipping for a quick glimpse of neat backyards, swimming pools, and houses of bewildering and conflicting architecture; now rushing through a new housing development or an area of blight, often paralleling the exuberance of newly planted trees. There is no immediacy of flagrant advertising, for signs and billboards are almost lost in the over-all blur.

Freeways allow the motorist to escape the confines of old streets which, in Los Angeles as in other cities, are merely channels between lines of telephone poles and squat buildings—streets too often bedeviled and defaced by gaudy and hideous advertising placards and defeating to the motorist with their continuous "Stop" and "Go." True, there are occasional strips or enclaves of delightful beauty, quiet streets of single-family homes protected by many shade trees and isolated from business thoroughfares. The freeways reveal a low-lying Los Angeles skyline, punctuated now with rapidly increasing "high-rise" structures in the "downtown," or "Central City," sections and in the Wilshire and Sunset Boulevard regions. The removal, in 1957, of height restrictions, imposed by officials who feared earthquakes, pointed the way to a lifting of the skyline. There are now forty- and fifty-story buildings in the embryo stage.

On breezeless, sunny days, a low-lying, yellowish-brown blanket of smog may be seen clinging to a horizon that presses closely in and blots out distance. The encircling mountains, no longer visible, seem to have trapped the fumes—the aerial garbage—of the city beneath the overlay of warm air. The sun has transformed these fumes—hydrocarbons and oxides of nitrogen—into smog. Nearly four

19

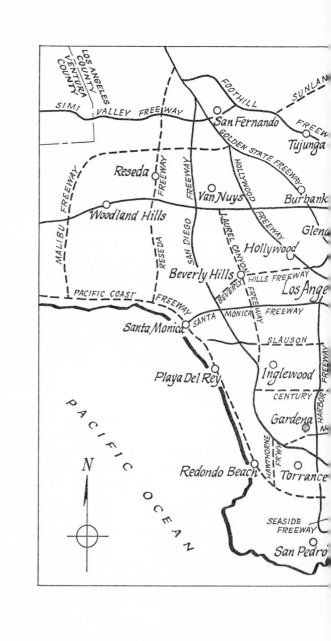

THE LOS ANGELES AREA showing principal freeways, constructed or projected, which interlink the supercity of 1980. Sections of Los Angeles, Orange, Ventura, and San Bernardino counties are involved. Municipal boundaries are excluded.

(Based on a map in *Westways Magazine*, June, 1965, copyright Automobile Club of Southern California.)

million automobile exhausts are the villains. Of the con-
taminates in Los Angeles County, 90 per cent is emitted by
motor vehicles. The remaining 10 per cent comes from
stationary sources. Early in the battle, industrial offenders
were muzzled, and since October, 1957, private incinera-
tors have been banned. Yet, on smoggy days the profile of
Los Angeles is stained—streaked and blurred. Visibility is
reduced, eyes smart, there is injury to sufferers from emphy-
sema, and plants and crops are damaged. Los Angeles does
not have noticeable smog every day, or every hour of a
smoggy day. Some sections rarely have smog. In other sections the residents know the hour smog will appear and just
when it will disappear. Actually, the mountains act as a flue
in a chimney, and during fall and early winter, when "Santa
Ana" winds blow, beaches and coastal districts may become
smoggier than the inland areas.

Since World War II, smog has been both a fact of Los
Angeles life and a political and polemical issue. In 1947 an
air pollution control program with an organization staffed
by experts to enforce decisions was launched by Los Angeles County. Millions of dollars have since been spent on
the Los Angeles program, which has been pointed to as an
example of a successful attempt in eliminating stationary
sources of air pollution. Today, county, state, and federal
agencies, along with the originally resistant Detroit makers
of automobiles and the great oil companies, work together
or in competition to stem and, hopefully, to eliminate the
air pollution caused by motor vehicles. They hope to ac-
complish this objective through appropriate legislation and
the perfection of exhaust devices on automobiles, even the
development of smog-free gasoline engines and fuel systems. Also, rapid transit systems are in the discussion stage.
Publicity seekers like to outdo each other in dire and often

conflicting predictions, for instance, that Angelenos are doomed to die in their aerial fumes.

When Los Angeles appeared to be the solitary sufferer from smog, other areas had no help to offer. Today, air pollution is recognized as an almost universal urban problem, and the campaign against the evil has taken on national proportions.

Many of us agree with Bill Henry, Los Angeles *Times* columnist, that the freeway system is the greatest thing that has happened to the city with the world's heaviest traffic. Engineers declare it to be the area's greatest achievement.

From no one point, not even from the highest jet plane, can all of Los Angeles be seen today. "Bits of it," wrote Sean O'Faolain in *Holiday*, "are always hidden even from the eye of the sun. Its populace can only get to know it, over the years, by taking it piecemeal in sampling tours, savoring gobbets of their vast urban universe like connoisseurs."

From the observation tower on the twenty-seventh floor of Los Angeles City Hall much of the rushing present can be seen, along with reminders of the past, for Los Angeles was born nearby, and intimations of the future. At first glance, the observer may see only the hundreds of parking lots crowded with the multicolored tops of parked automobiles. There seem to be more parking lots than buildings. Or he may watch the flow of traffic on the Hollywood-San Bernardino Freeway where it intersects with the traffic tides of the Harbor and Pasadena freeways.

This first impression is of a Los Angeles dominated by the automobile and made fluid by the freeway. The view encompasses only part of downtown Los Angeles or Central City, and the greatest activity in this area is to the south and west of City Hall.

Looking westward, the Civic Center can be seen, a region

of government buildings extending from the City Hall almost to Harbor Freeway. It lies in the heart of the land of the old pueblo. There, almost in final form, a group of functional structures—city, county, state, and federal—have arisen. Topping the slope are the three buildings comprising the Music Center for the Performing Arts and the climactic structure belonging to the Department of Water and Power. The latter building, named for architectural honors by a two-man jury of architects, was described as bringing "life and direction to the city after dark,"—for by night it is a giant lighting fixture. In the Civic Center's midst is the mall, rising in tiers and decorated with plantings and playing fountains.

Immediately adjoining the Civic Center on the west is the largely denuded Bunker Hill, a region being slowly transformed, under federal and municipal redevelopment action, into a towering business, shopping, and residential area which will most certainly be a fantastic addition to the skyline. Bunker Hill in the 1880's and 1890's was a favorite residential district, its Victorian mansions overlooking what was then the business section of Los Angeles. As a nostalgic memento of that time, the funicular railway, Angels Flight, carrying passengers up and down Bunker Hill, has survived and is being incorporated into the planning of the Community Redevelopment Agency.

Spring Street, extending to the south from City Hall, is a part of the financial center of Los Angeles, lined by banks, trust companies, insurance concerns, and the Los Angeles Stock Exchange. No longer confined to one street, however, newer financial buildings are rising to the south and west in a fury of construction along intersecting Sixth Street and Wilshire Boulevard, as well as Figueroa Street. Wilshire Boulevard, extending seventeen miles from the downtown area to the Santa Monica shore, has become the home of a series of clustered insurance and banking buildings, especially in the Ambassador Hotel region and in the Beverly Hills and Westwood areas.

Looking north from the observation tower through the grim jungle of low buildings, railroad tracks, warehouses, gas tanks, and stubby streets, it is possible to see a long, cement-lined channel crossed by occasional bridges. This channel keeps prisoner the unseen trickle of the Los Angeles River. For thousands, probably millions, of years this river found its way into the Los Angeles basin from the north, flowing through a land then thick with willows and sycamores. This river was instrumental in shaping the area. When it neared the ocean, it used now one mouth, now another, or merely flooded the landscape. In pre-Spanish days it drew the Shoshoneans, who established villages such as Yang-na—its site close to the present-day City Hall. The people of this village came forth in 1769 to greet the first party of Spanish explorers, who, so the Indians said, had "nasty, white color and . . . ugly blue eyes." The Los Angeles River drew the founders of the farming village that became Los Angeles. Before flood-control days, the river often became, in rainy seasons, a raging turmoil of purple waters. A reminder of the founding days is the gray-green, circular cluster of trees that marks the surviving plaza of the Spanish and Mexican pueblo—very close to the location of the first plaza. The old plaza district, the birthplace of Los Angeles, is being slowly, very slowly, regenerated under a master plan developed by the state, the county, and the city to preserve or re-create something of the Spanish, Mexican, and early Anglo years.

The view of Los Angeles from an airplane can be exhilarating. On a smoggy or foggy day, Los Angeles, seen from

25

above, may be a colossal murk, above which a plane must circle and re-circle while waiting for the signal to land at Los Angeles International Airport. On a clear day, however, the city takes on the quality of a many-hued counterpane laced with freeways and enlivened with the sparkle of swimming pools. Instead of vast rectangular patterns, the freeways are curving forms that embrace buildings of every sort—electronic centers, supermarkets, golf courses, and innumerable subdivisions. By night the approaches to the city, especially those from Las Vegas and San Bernardino County, appear to be almost continuous, bejeweled tapestries.

Does the profile of Los Angeles, when seen from freeways or airways, suggest that the area is becoming the "prototype of the supercity," the "ultimate city," or the "living laboratory" for the urban observer? Possibly a closer study of the development of the explosive, motorized city will give an answer.

4

Motorized City

IN THE EARLY 1920's, sardonic visitors to Southern California began describing Los Angeles as "six suburbs in search of a city." Later the number became ninety or one hundred. Many of these newcomers thought they had originated the clever description. Unwittingly, they had been inspired by an internationally successful play, the product of Italian dramatist Luigi Pirandello. This play, launched in 1921, bore the title *Six Characters in Search of an Author*.

The "search-for-a-city" appellation became partly accurate in the 1920's, for Los Angeles, spread-eagling in all directions, gradually ceased having a day-and-night center in a single, active, downtown district. For a score of years visitors reached this downtown center from nearby towns by using the convenient red cars of Henry E. Huntington's Pacific Electric Railway. Once in the downtown district, visitors transacted business on three parallel streets—Main, Spring, and Broadway, and their connectives. East Fifth Street should perhaps be included. Prior to the 1920's, this area had been alive during the day and evening hours with people, shops, stores, excellent restaurants, theaters, and churches. Saloons were numerous and heavily patronized.

27

Among the favorite spots for the male of the sporting set was Jim Jeffries' place on Spring Street. Neon lights blazed gaudily to advertise the local beers and current shows. Dance halls, usually upstairs in this or nearby areas, were popular.

Such was the "central city" of the early 1900's—the place Angelenos and visitors went for business and fun. Main Street itself—today largely skid row—was so gay and so gaudy a stretch between First and Eighth streets, with the added attractions of burlesque houses and the eye-dazzling advertisements of men's medical specialists, that a national magazine devoted a feature article to its exuberance.

Before the 1920's were over, however, this downtown area, under the impact of the automobile, was changing radically. Stores dared to establish outlying branches near the newer subdivisions. Existing restaurants and theaters lost patrons to competitors closer to the thousands of tile-roofed homes that had been built farther and ever farther from the old center. The rapid-transit system, losing constantly to the private automobile, was little by little curtailing its services. A whole series of new centers of business and other neighborhood facilities had arisen in hitherto unsubdivided areas, leaving the downtown area as a core for specialized activities, largely financial and headquarters enterprises. The automobile, available to almost everyone, was the determining factor in the establishment of new residential and business sections.

Although Los Angeles was changing, the city did not lose its "downtown" or "core." Rather, the character of downtown changed. Aging buildings gave way to parking lots, but the first-class structures remained, and still remain, with public patronage limited largely to daytime hours.

The expansive growth and decentralization of Los Angeles began with the coming of the automobile. In 1921 a farsighted individual named A. W. Ross had a hunch that the automobile, the newest method of transportation, would change America's living and shopping habits. Accordingly, he bought eighteen strategic acres of land in the Los Angeles area—on a narrow lane called Wilshire. The tract was halfway between the town and the beach. It was within easy reach, by automobile, of the westernmost district of Los Angeles and of youthful Beverly Hills. This was the beginning of the so-called "Miracle Mile." Wilshire Boulevard developed into one of the greatest business thoroughfares in the West. Ultimately, the boulevard extended from the historic core of the city to the sea at Santa Monica. When spectacular architectural developments took place at various points in Los Angeles, Beverly Hills, Westwood, and other areas, the prospect that Wilshire would become a continuous canyon of high-rise structures was apparent.

In tribute to the vision of A. W. Ross, a bronze bust of him was placed in a grassy triangle at Wilshire Boulevard and Curson Avenue. Yet Ross is only a symbol of a movement that began in the early 1920's, which transformed Los Angeles into what it is today and what it may be tomorrow. Many other A. W. Rosses were at work in the early years of the 1920's, in all the areas surrounding the original four square leagues that had sufficed Los Angeles since pueblo days.

Some writers seem to think of Los Angeles as being always in a state of boom. That assumption is not technically true. The peak or boom years in real estate activity— notably in Southern California—have come approximately every seventeen or twenty years, that is, a generation apart. The high points in real estate sales, it is noted, have been 1855, 1875, 1887, 1906, 1923, 1946, and 1963. The down

29

swings of the cycle have been somewhat modified in the Los Angeles area by the continued upsurge of population.

Between 1920 and 1924, the pull of the boom drew at least one hundred thousand people a year to Los Angeles alone. During that period almost every piece of acreage in the area encircling the old city was ablaze with rows of red and yellow flags bearing a variety of cheerful messages: "Water? Yes," "Sewers? Yes," "It's a Steal," and "Sold, Sold, Sold." Ambitious white-collar clerks everywhere deserted office jobs to become real estate salesmen.

Every state in the Union contributed to the western migration during this period. For the first time, the migration was by automobile—a fact that distinguished this boom from preceding booms. Half a million people from Illinois, Texas, Missouri, New York, and Iowa went west. This mass movement was mostly composed of men and women under the age of thirty-five who were seeking jobs and homes. They found both. The number of building permits issued in Los Angeles during 1923 were exceeded only by the number issued in New York and Chicago. Free bus trips and free lunches lured buyers to remote subdivisions, where they were destined to hear hypnotic sales talks and to sign on the dotted line.

Los Angeles, relying increasingly on the automobile, fanned out in all directions and became a city of suburbs. Valleys, hillsides, deserts, and seacoast provided sites for thousands of new homes, usually of stucco with red-tiled roofs. Ultimately, the suburbs themselves expanded, absorbing the remaining open spaces, until Los Angeles took on the dimensions of a spread-eagled giant. The growing population made necessary business and governmental expansion and a network of utility lines and highways designed

30

for the use and the convenience of automobile drivers. The supermarket, the shopping center, Sunday and twenty-four-hour stores, the drive-in theater and bank—all came into existence, developed, became normal, and established new patterns of activity for the nation. Under a program begun in 1895, the physical boundaries of the municipality of Los Angeles had expanded through annexation and consolidation. Finally, the original 28 square miles with which the pueblo started had become more than 450.

In the boom of the twenties, the potentialities of Wilshire Boulevard had caused a downtown department store, Bullock's, to pioneer in the construction of a large, all-modern branch on the far west side of the city in a non-business area on the boulevard. A procession of department stores, which continued to maintain headquarters in the old downtown district, followed Bullock's example. They moved not only to Wilshire Boulevard but also to strategic street intersections and to other communities and towns in the Los Angeles area. This building of branch establishments in regions of potential growth has continued to the present day and has contributed to the rise of lush business centers in the counties adjoining or near Los Angeles County.

Another development during the boom of the twenties was the rapid spread of branch banking. The neighborhood branch bank, with its headquarters downtown, satisfied the banking needs of homeowners in a myriad of new subdivisions. It also offered escrow service to customers who found it inconvenient to visit downtown banks and title insurance companies when buying, selling, or financing real estate. Bilateral representation by a bank or title insurance concern, carrying out the wishes of both sides in a land "deal," became established practice in Southern California.

31

"Going into escrow," "escrowing a deal," or "signing escrow instructions" were phrases common to practically every adult Angeleno and Southern Californian.

The diminution of night life in downtown Los Angeles was evidenced in the closing, one by one, of the area's restaurants and theaters. Main Street took on an increasing drabness, a development that transformed its saloons into B-girl hangouts and ultimately resulted in a full-fledged skid row. The patrons of the remaining saloons and burlesque houses were usually the inhabitants of the nearby flophouses, once nice hotels.

The noisy closing, on December 31, 1953, of the Good Fellows Grotto at 341 South Main Street, which had resisted the change to the last, symbolized the final passing of downtown night life. This restaurant, established in 1905, had been the favored haunt of theater crowds, actors, actresses, and the sporting element. But its neighborhood had so deteriorated that diners could no longer be induced to seek out this last place of good food and good drink. Its most conspicuous neighbor was the dilapidated Follies Theater, a burlesque establishment which managed to survive through the gaudiness of its advertising. The luncheon crowd at the Grotto was not big enough to pay costs. The final printed menu of this "grill and oyster house" was labeled "The Restful Charm of the Gay Nineties in the 'Atomic Fifties.' " From noon on, during December 31, 1953, the place, with its cubbyhole dining rooms and the lingering staleness of its air, was crowded with farewell diners. That day the Grotto did a roaring business in food and drink, with souvenir hunters taking everything they could lay their hands on. Famous for its superlative Hangtown Fries, an early-day California specialty, the Grotto saw a mighty scramble for the last two fries made by the departing chef. I consumed one of the two.

Expansion and refinement of the features of suburban development have characterized Los Angeles in the decades since the twenties. When a market or supermarket was started in a strategic area, there would grow about it a community of shops and stores. A more recent trend has been the development of whole planned communities or "cities" within the limits of the larger city or just outside. The planning of these communities calls for architects conscious of the needs of open spaces, parks, schools, single-family homes, apartment houses, markets, restaurants, and other private and public expressions of modern living. "Century City," within Los Angeles and adjoining Beverly Hills, is an example, occupying a huge area formerly used by Twentieth Century-Fox studios.

Downtown Los Angeles, after a long period of lethargy, is now springing to furious life with high-rise buildings of forty, fifty, or more stories completed, under construction, or planned. Central City is coming into its own. Towering banks, savings and loan structures, insurance company buildings, and oil company headquarters form a dramatic urban core. Their existence emphasizes the need for a long-overdue rapid transit system that can assume part of the load of the private automobile, existing bus lines, and proliferating freeways. Even the skid row area is receiving attention from planners, who foresee its transformation into an integral part of Central City. So, too, "Little Tokyo," in the shadow of the City Hall, is now an ambitious section of wide, busy streets and substantial business buildings, the country's largest center of Japanese-American activity outside of the Hawaiian Islands.

Central City and the whole of Los Angeles are encircled by the freeways which made the area mobile. Angelenos love "the world's most ambitious freeway system," especially if they are under the age of sixty-five. They are excited by the completion of each new link in the gigantic program, which may be completed in 1980 or 1990. They are soothed, as they drive, by reporters in helicopters who scan freeways from above and pass along vital messages about traffic situations. Despite the frequent traffic jams, despite the demands on every driver's nervous system, and despite the smog, citizens enjoy the ease of getting anywhere quickly. They enjoy the "daily joust with Fate."

In 1967, seven million Los Angeles County residents were driving 3,700,000 automobiles. The only protest from these people is made when a planned freeway is scheduled to go through their own homes or property, or when a park or a historic area is threatened for destruction by the apparently omnipotent State Highway Commission, which plans its freeways with deadly inevitability.

5

Hollywood Impact

HOLLYWOOD, WHICH HAS exerted so extraordinary an effect on Los Angeles, on the nation, and on the world, is always being defined.

Geographically, Hollywood's boundaries are today completely elastic. "Hollywood is no longer a piece of geography," writes Charles Champlin, entertainment editor of the Los Angeles *Times*, "but a symbolic handle for American film-making, which is itself a worldwide activity."

Hollywood is still often referred to as that section of Los Angeles in which the American motion picture industry was originally centered. But the word came to mean any place in Southern California where motion picture people lived and worked, whether in Los Angeles, Culver City, Beverly Hills, Santa Monica, Malibu, or the San Fernando Valley. It could cross a county line to Conejo Valley in Ventura County, where Metro-Goldwyn-Mayer, at the moment wanting to move from its Culver City lot, plans to build a new thirty-million-dollar complex that will include administration offices, film laboratories, theaters, and sound stages.

Hollywood, in the expanded use of the word, years ago became more than a physical region. Broadly, it may refer

35

to the American motion picture industry itself or to the life or world of that industry. Moreover, "Hollywood" has become, like the advertising man's "Madison Avenue," a mildly uncomplimentary term summing up a way of life or a point of view. To "go Hollywood," for example, means to become egocentric, affected, or insincere in manner. "Hollywood," as an adjective, may connote something gaudy, loud, flashy, vulgar, mediocre, or sporty.

Hollywood started as a subdivision in Cahuenga Valley, part of the promotional parceling of acreage during Southern California's fantastic real estate boom of 1887–88. The name "Hollywood" appeared on a colorful, ornamental map of this subdivision. The map, about three feet square, had provision for twenty-five blocks. On the map the handsome "Hotel Hollywood," the ample residence of promoter Horace H. Wilcox, the Pacific Ocean, and the beautifully green Cahuenga Pass were shown, with mountains looming in the rear. A legend on the map urged those interested to apply to the office of founder Wilcox, located on Spring Street in Los Angeles. Mrs. Wilcox is credited with naming the subdivision. The name was that of a summer home owned by a chance acquaintance who lived near Chicago.

Hollywood, the subdivision, was a success. It enlarged its boundaries and incorporated in 1903. As a small farm area, it continued to supply Los Angeles with watermelons, tomatoes, green peppers, and other fruits and vegetables. By 1910, the year the make-believe industry came to Hollywood, the place had five thousand people and needed more water and an outfall sewer. Los Angeles offered both, and a consolidation resulted.

In the fall of 1910, a tavern and barn at the corner of Sunset Boulevard and Gower Street became Hollywood's first movie studio. David Horsley, president of the Nestor

Film Company, was the first individual to produce a motion picture in the region called Hollywood, though Colonel William Selig and D. W. Griffith were already shooting pictures in non-Hollywood areas.

The history of Hollywood and its film-making has been told many times. It is enough to say that by the early 1940's Hollywood was the film center, producing 90 per cent of all the motion pictures made in America and supplying most of the pictures shown throughout the world. The age of munificence, as it has been called, ended with the advent of television, but the rivalry between movies and television has now given way to a profitable coexistence. Television took up the slack when the production of movies dropped.

Charles Champlin, in the December 24, 1966, issue of *Saturday Review*, had this to say of Hollywood's restoration to economic good health: "Through its outright sales of old films to television, through its leasing of films to television, through its production of all those series, and now through its production of features for TV, Hollywood is notably enriched—financially if not qualitatively—by the medium. Indeed, the recent rapid-fire takeover of several studios by outside financial interests reflects in considerable part an awareness of the television gold yet to be mined."

In the last decade, "run-away production" has not only been one of Hollywood's principal topics of conversation, it has changed the face of Hollywood. An increasing number of pictures have been made in England, France, Germany, Italy, and Spain, although largely with American financing. Director Otto Preminger reacted by saying, in December, 1961, that "the people in Hollywood can only save Hollywood by making it more productive, by having a more positive approach, by competing with the outside world, by opening up this industry to young people, by making Hollywood a place that creative people would want to come to."

The practice of making movies in Europe has been and is profitable because of lower labor costs, government subsidies, and freedom from unco-operative unions. European film-makers have become increasingly experienced, and their growing technical sophistication threatens Hollywood's position as the world's film center. Sometimes it is in Rome, sometimes in London, where the talent pool of the better directors, writers, and artists seems to be concentrated. However, European labor costs are rising. Over the years, Hollywood may continue to stage comebacks.

Again quoting Charles Champlin, in the March 27, 1967, issue of the Los Angeles *Times*, "Hollywood is no longer an enclave, a walled city defensive and grimly resisting the new waves from elsewhere. Hollywood, too, is an open city, beckoning the new talents from abroad. Beckoning, even more startling, the new talents from at home, the youngsters who have proved themselves on campus or in the documentary or industrial fields." This statement would indicate that the Hollywood of 1967 was nearing the situation called for six years earlier by Preminger.

Over the years, another threat to Hollywood has been the attempts made by various American cities to lure the film-making industry away from Los Angeles—San Francisco and New York are both guilty. To combat the latest attempt made by New York, Mayor Sam Yorty of Los Angeles is planning a 740-acre motion picture and television city in Los Angeles to "insure Hollywood's world leadership of the film and broadcasting arts."

Hollywood's motion pictures have had a revolutionary effect on Southern California, on the United States, and on the world. No other medium of communication has so stirred the senses, tastes, attitudes, desires, and customs of people throughout the towns and cities of the world.

Ever since Marlene Dietrich launched womankind into the wearing of pants, Hollywood has influenced fashion. Hollywood has even determined love-making techniques. Hollywood films, showing luxurious ways of living, have caused low-income groups to be filled with envy or ambition. Whole nations have been moved to adapt or imitate alleged American customs and Americanisms. The "Hun-Hate" pictures, during and following World Wars I and II, kept many Germans from visiting the United States. Movies have made some Europeans think of America as a country of crime and horror, but surveys by the United States Information Agency seem to find that American films are now creating a favorable impression overseas. The world-wide popularity of "Westerns" has caused European and Asiatic film-makers to produce their own brand of cowboy pictures. About the universal popularity of American movies, there can be no doubt. And the great educational value of documentary films is recognized at home and abroad. Such films are potentially a vital part of the teaching function in industry and in schools of all levels.

Hollywood's pictures have made Los Angeles a mecca for countless thousands of young people wanting a career in the motion picture industry. They have drawn to Los Angeles novelists, musicians, dancers, photographers, and technicians from the countries of the world. When Hollywood was turning out four hundred movies a year, the interest in the people and the products of Hollywood was so universal that several hundred feature writers were assigned to Hollywood to report its happenings.

The widespread appeal and influence of motion pictures are indicated by the huge outpouring of books about Holly-

39

wood since the 1920's. The book titles are numbered in the thousands, without including the foreign language publications. Hundreds of books have been written concerning the technical phases of film-making. There are also many nontechnical books: general and selective histories, biographies, autobiographies, commentaries, and confessions of columnists, legmen, and prostitutes. Five hundred or more novels have been written using Hollywood settings. Many of these nontechnical books are of interest because they tell the story of an industry and a region which has so greatly influenced the world.

Terry Ramsaye's vivid and journalistic *A Million and One Nights* (1926) and Benjamin B. Hampton's carefully wrought *A History of the Movies* (1931) continue to be the basic histories. Arthur Knight's panoramic, spirited, and scholarly *The Liveliest Art* (1957), which traces the story of the motion picture and of Hollywood from the beginning days into the television era, is of extreme importance. Knight's volume, if updated, could well be the most useful book on Hollywood yet written. Another good book, for those who prefer their history in fictional form, is Robert Carson's dog-eat-dog novel of Hollywood, *The Magic Lantern* (1952), covering the period from the time of the nickelodeon to the introduction of sound pictures.

Among the 275 or more biographies and autobiographies of film celebrities may be found the greatest number of "non-books." Yet Theodore Huff's *Charlie Chaplin* (1951) is a fascinating and understanding account of Hollywood's greatest actor. It is the best of the many Chaplin books— even better than Chaplin's *My Autobiography* (1964).

Life stories, in book form, are available of Mary Astor, George Burns, Bette Davis, Dale Evans, Roy Rogers, Douglas Fairbanks, Sr., and Douglas Fairbanks, Jr., Eva

Gabor, Elinor Glynn, Jean Harlow, Hedda Hopper, Lou-ella Parsons, Erich Von Stroheim, Carl Laemmle, Harold Lloyd, Victor McLaglen, "Groucho" Marx, Margaret O'Brien, Lillian Gish, the Talmadge sisters, Mae West, Greta Garbo, Lita Grey Chaplin, Adolph Zukor, and almost any other film celebrity one might name. The accomplishments of a celebrity, whether presented by the author or a ghost-writer, rarely justifies the publication of a book; yet, to the regional historian it may yield pay dirt.

A fresh look at the landscape and the people of Hollywood can be found in Gavin Lambert's *The Slide Area: Scenes of Hollywood Life* (1960). Lambert, an English script writer and novelist of subtle perception, depicts the odd-balls on the fringes of the film world. The resulting somewhat fragmentary studies hang together like the elements of a good abstraction.

Gene Fowler's books, especially *Good Night, Sweet Prince: The Life and Times of John Barrymore* (1944) and *Minutes of the Last Meeting* (1954), both devoted to comic, lusty, and grim Hollywood adventures, offer superb entertainment. Another entertaining book is Errol Flynn's plush account of roistering Hollywood, *My Wicked, Wicked Ways* (1960). The brothers William C. and Cecil B. de Mille have contributed to the Hollywood story in their books. Leo C. Rosten's important book, *Hollywood: The Movie Colony, The Movie Makers* (1941), is a gossipless dissection of the activities and problems of producers, actors, directors, and writers. Edward Wagenknecht's *The Movies in the Age of Innocence* (1962) is a significant study of the silent movies.

Bosley Crowther's *The Lion's Share* (1957), the story of Metro-Goldwyn-Mayer, is both a history of and a commentary on the film industry. He does a better job in this book

41

than in his later and franker *Hollywood Rajah: The Life and Times of Louis B. Mayer* (1966). In *King Cohn* (1967), by Bob Thomas, the long-time head of Columbia Pictures, Harry Cohn, is given full treatment. Cohn has been described by many. Budd Schulberg called Cohn "the Horatio Alger of the four-letter word." Hedda Hopper named him "a sadistic sonofabitch." Others have recognized his extraordinary activities as a "womanizer" and the producer of some of the best and most successful pictures ever made.

A revealing, amusing, and sophisticated analysis of the Hollywood inhabitants, written in the manner of a scientific study of a primitive society, is Hortense Powdermaker's *Hollywood, the Dream Factory: An Anthropologist Looks at the Movie-Makers* (1951). Miss Powdermaker finds that the South Sea natives have classified American movies into two types—"kiss-kiss" and "bang-bang," love and violence. In her chapter "Habitat and People, Mythical and Real," she discovers that Hollywood dominates Los Angeles. Hollywood, she says, "is engaged in the mass production of prefabricated daydreams." In her chapter on "Taboos," she finds that "every part of movie production is circumscribed by a very special code of taboos." In "Front Office" she discusses the power situation. Throughout her study, Dr. Powdermaker uses anthropological references familiar in popular lingo. In her comparison with the Maori, she learns that the "in-group is an autocracy, dependent, in part, on biological relationships."

Novels about Hollywood, beginning with Harry Leon Wilson's still tragi-comic *Merton of the Movies* (1922), are continually written. Carl Van Vechten's *Spider Boy* (1928) is the prototype of later satires which tell of fabulous pay to transplanted authors who do no work. After all these years the label "best" still adheres, in my opinion, to Budd Schulberg's *What Makes Sammy Run?* (1941), the story of the super-aggressive Sammy Glick who rises to the top of the heap in a now dated Hollywood world. The status of the Schulberg novel is sometimes challenged by critics who prefer F. Scott Fitzgerald's unfinished *The Last Tycoon* (1941) and, illogically, Nathaniel West's *The Day of the Locust* (1939).

6

Minority Report

RACIAL TENSIONS have existed in Los Angeles at least since the middle 1830's. They have been highlighted by explosive and disgraceful incidents involving various races and nationalities. A review of these affairs may be pertinent to the still much discussed "Watts" riots and to the racial and national tensions that still exist.

In 1830, a Los Angeles census counted 764 whites and 198 Indians living within the pueblo itself. The Indian elements included possibly a handful of people who were descendants of the inhabitants of the original prehistoric village of Yang-na; the majority, however, were mission and non-mission Indians who had come into town to work. Alcalde Vicente Sanchez, commenting on his census report, said that "the heathen of the neighborhood, who come here and work with the whites, are treated well and live a civilized and quiet life."

This happy picture presently changed. Secularization of the missions of California—abrupt transfer from church to lay administration—brought the more irresponsible Indians to Los Angeles. Secularization was accomplished between 1834 and 1836, causing a substantial increase in the pueblo's Indian population, so much that in 1836 the Indians of the area were placed in a segregated district located near the present corner of Commercial and Alameda streets. This *"ranchería* of *poblanos,"* as it was called, existed for ten years.

From their makeshift huts these motley Indians went forth to work, get drunk, and become a nuisance to the whites. For ten years the Indian problem was before the city council. One important complaint was that the Indians bathed and washed in the principal canal or *zanja* which brought citizens their drinking water. By the end of 1845, the council yielded to pressure and relocated the Indians across the river. The new Indian village, because of its isolation, was worse than the old. Indians stole fences, so it was alleged, got unbearably drunk, and spread venereal diseases. In the latter part of 1846, the American soldiers under Captain Gillespie liked to spend their evenings in the Indian village, a mile from headquarters. A year later, to end the discordant gatherings, the council ordered the village razed. Thereafter, employers of Indian servants were expected to be responsible for their shelter and care.

By the time American administration had been organized in 1850, however, a different Indian problem had developed. There were four thousand "domesticated Indians" in the county of Los Angeles. On weekends Los Angeles streets swarmed with Indians. On one occasion, following a game of *peón*, a fight between San Luis Rey Indians and Cahuillas from San Bernardino Valley on the hill behind the plaza church resulted in at least fifty deaths. Arrests for drunkenness and disorderly conduct were normal and numerous. City prisoners were assembled in chain gangs and "occupied in public work." The material for chain gangs—Indians—was so ample that the council took an-

45

other step on August 16, 1850, providing that Indian prisoners could be auctioned off to the highest bidder for private service.

Since the pay for the almost-free labor was apt to be in *aguardiente*, the Indians of Los Angeles gradually died out. On-the-spot-observer Horace Bell, in his *Reminiscences of a Ranger*, wrote: "Los Angeles had its slave mart as well as New Orleans and Constantinople—only the slave at Los Angeles was sold fifty-two times a year as long as he lived, which did not generally exceed one, two or three years, under the new dispensation . . . . Thousands of honest, useful people were absolutely destroyed in this way."

Weekly auctions took place in Los Angeles until as late as 1869, but the shortage of workers, caused by the high death rate of Indians, resulted in abandoned vineyards, neglected fruit orchards, and a suffering municipal water system.

With Anglo-Americans pouring into Los Angeles in the 1850's, a new type of tension developed, this time between the English-speaking newcomers and the Spanish-speaking *Californios* and newly arrived Sonorans. The former, the "Anglos," made up the minority group—in 1851 they comprised about one-tenth of the three thousand Angelenos—but they brought with them their prejudices against the people they called "Spaniards." The *Californios* and Sonorans, on their part, were jealous of the ambitious and forthright Anglos who soon set about taking over the ranchos and governmental activities.

The clashing emotions of the two peoples from two distinct cultures were evident in the famous Lugo case of 1851–52. Two members of a long prominent, Californian, ranch-owning family were charged with a murder which was never to be solved. Angelenos took sides in the Lugo case largely according to each individual's national origin. Similarly, when gambler Dave Brown was about to be lynched—hanged to the cross-beam of a Los Angeles corral gateway—his final statement was that he did not mind being hanged but did not want it done by "greasers." The mob, composed mostly of Mexicans, accommodated Brown by allowing him the luxury of an "all-American" hanging. Los Angeles in the 1850's was overrun by outlaws and gamblers, many of them the victims of anti-"foreign" legislation, and activities in the Mother Lode. These men swelled the gangs of dark-skinned, embittered outcasts who robbed and killed in Southern California. The lynching of Mexicans accused of crime was commonplace in Los Angeles during the 1850's and was in part attributable to racial or nationalistic animosities.

Anti-Chinese sentiment had been developing throughout California during the Gold Rush period. It found climactic expression in Los Angeles on a day in October, 1871, in a dreadful outburst of mob violence. Chinatown, in Los Angeles, had been expanding in the late 1860's. Finally, it took over the section immediately east of the plaza and extended along both sides of Alameda Street. This closely packed area offered color, gaiety, mystery, and vice to visitors and a place to live and a way of life for Chinese. When city policemen tried to break up disorders resulting from a tong war started by the abduction of a woman, a policeman, his brother, and an assistant were shot. A white mob quickly formed. In spite of the efforts of the sheriff and other officials, the riot spread. The mob surrounded "Nigger Alley," adjoining Chinatown, where they smashed roofs and buildings and beat and hanged twenty-two or more Chinese.

Naturally there were national and international repercussions. Locally, however, nothing was done about the

47

mob's actions. On the contrary, the coroner's jury found that the victims died of strangulation at the hands of parties unknown. When suits were brought against Los Angeles under a statute making cities responsible for damage done by mobs and riots, the ruling of the California Supreme Court was adverse. As explained in Leon Thomas David's *Law and Lawyers*, "The claim of the Chinese for injury to their property was defeated on the ground that they failed to notify the Mayor of the impending riot and that their conduct had precipitated it."

The Mexican contribution to the population of Los Angeles, like that of the Negroes, began with the pueblo's founding and has continued ever since. By the time of World War II, the city had several hundred thousand Mexican-Americans. They or their parents or grandparents had come to California, especially during the period from 1910 to 1930, to work in the fields, in the orange groves, or on the railroads. In Los Angeles these people, mostly a low-income, frustrated group, gradually took over certain older sections of the city, often "poverty pockets." They retained some of their customs, their language, and their religious beliefs—modified by contact and competition with other Angelenos. The younger generation found life a mixture of difficult problems, including the fact of discrimination in certain areas of activity.

The climax to this potentially dangerous situation came in 1942–43, partly as a result of the growth of "Pachuco" gangs among some of the younger Mexican-Americans and of the policy of mass arrests by local police when fights took place. Los Angeles newspapers gave such sensational publicity to gangland incidents and arrests that the publicity assumed the nature of anti-Mexican propaganda. "As the tension grew in the Mexican colony," wrote Beatrice Griffith in her *American Me*, "war workers, servicemen and law-abiding citizens felt that they were being engulfed by a Mexican crime wave." Many of the young Mexican-American men had taken to ducktail haircuts and zoot-suits, highlighted by long coats draped in the rear and by flaring, bell-bottom trousers. This garb made them conspicuous on the streets and became symbolic of what most Angelenos disliked.

The so-called zoot-suit riots broke out early in June, 1943, preceded by clashes at Venice and Santa Monica between sailors and Mexican-American patrons of beach dance halls. Full-scale rioting broke out over one week end, with mob action taking on some resemblance to the anti-Chinese affair of 1871. Sailors, marines, soldiers, and civilians invaded the Mexican areas of Los Angeles. As described in *American Me*, "Mexican American boys (and some Negro) were dragged from theaters, stripped of their clothing, beaten and left naked on the streets. Later they were taken to jail by the police, 'who cleaned up the Pachuco debris in the wake of the sailors.'" Young men "were dragged out of restaurants and off streetcars, mauled and beaten by the yelling mob." For four nights, warfare between the zoot-suiters and the servicemen, joined by large numbers of civilians, continued furiously. Theaters, poolrooms, dance halls in the so-called Mexican area, and homes "were invaded in the hunt for Mexican and Negro boys wearing zootsuits." The end came soon after one thousand policemen were sent into the warring areas and when, on June 8, Los Angeles was declared out of bounds to naval personnel.

Part of the tension existing among Mexican-Americans and others arose from the mass arrests and mass trial that followed the murder of a young man named José Díaz. The

49

body of Díaz had been picked up on the night of August 2, 1942, near a mudhole called "Sleepy Lagoon," a place used as a swimming pool in Southeast Los Angeles. His skull had been fractured, and the condition of the face and fists indicated that Díaz had been in a fight. The alcohol in his blood showed a state of near intoxication. Earlier in the evening there had been a fight at the Lagoon between Mexican groups or gangs. In mass raids the police arrested three hundred Mexican-Americans. Of these, twenty-three were indicted and placed on trial for first degree murder. Seventeen were convicted of "varying degrees of responsibility." The aftermath, to quote Carey McWilliams in his *Southern California County*, was that "eighteen months later an appellate court reversed the conviction and severely castigated the trial judge and the prosecution for the methods which had been used to secure the verdict." The mystery of the Díaz death was never solved.

World War II also provided the background for other explosions of racial tensions. In the summer of 1942, about 110,000 West Coast Japanese—75,000 of them American citizens and a large proportion of them Southern Californians—were relocated in concentration camps called "relocation centers." These people were removed from their homes and places of business and put under guard in camps authorized by President Roosevelt and the War Department. Today the whole story of this misadventure is most repellent to Californians. At the time, however, with Pearl Harbor a recent hideous memory, Californians were strongly in favor of the action. Attorney General, later Governor and now Chief Justice, Earl Warren favored the removal, as did many others, like Walter Lippman, who have since acquired the reputations of being "liberals." Even the Supreme Court upheld the action. Until 1945, the uprooted

Japanese families, who were forced to sell their homes and properties at a fraction of their value and were then shipped off to barracks, worked and lived in discomfort, though without oppression. The victims have since made a noteworthy comeback as citizens, although they received only partial compensation for losses, and this through the 1948 Evacuation Repayment Act. Nevertheless, the United States government did recognize that a dreadful mistake had been made.

Los Angeles' worst race riot—the so-called Watts Riot—took place during six days of August, 1965, when ten thousand Negroes, in menacing, marauding bands, took to the streets of south-central Los Angeles. "They looted stores, set fires, beat up white passers-by whom they hauled from stopped cars, many of which were turned upside down and burned, exchanged shots with law enforcement officers, and stoned and shot at firemen . . . . Ultimately an area covering 465 square miles had to be controlled with the aid of military authority before public order was restored . . . . When the spasm passed, thirty-four persons were dead, and the wounded and hurt numbered 1,032 more. Property damage was about $40,000,000. Arrested for one crime or another were 3,952 persons, women as well as men, including over 500 youths under eighteen."

The quotations are from the official and masterly summing up of the dreadful affair, *Violence In the City—An End Or A Beginning?* the report made by a commission appointed by Governor Brown and headed by John A. McCone.

As in earlier outbursts of extreme racial feeling in Los Angeles, the 1965 riots were related directly to a minority-group population explosion. Negroes in Los Angeles County increased in number from 75,000 in 1940 to 650,000 in

51

1965, almost a tenfold jump. Two-thirds of the Negro population lived in the area involved in the rioting—perhaps not a slum in the Harlem sense, but a crowded region greatly in need of upgrading and renewal. The community of Watts was not the actual point of origin of the outbreak, but its business streets bore the brunt of the riots. Until 1926, when Watts was annexed to Los Angeles, the population was largely Caucasian. Negroes began moving in from the South to be employed by the Pacific Electric Railway Company, their housing furnished by the company.

The arrest of a drunken Negro youth at seven o'clock on August 11, 1965—an extremely humid Wednesday night—triggered the violent actions of the Negro mobs. The fury spread, and by early Friday rioters had begun burning blocks on 103d Street in Watts and were driving off firemen by sniper fire and rock throwing. By late afternoon mob activity had penetrated fifty or sixty blocks to the north. Throughout all of Los Angeles, white citizens were buying guns. Not until ten o'clock Friday evening did the first contingents of the National Guard reach the riot area. By midnight, they were marching shoulder to shoulder clearing the streets. They worked in co-ordination with the various law enforcement agencies—policemen, sheriff's officers, highway patrolmen, city marshals, and firemen. Looting, burning, shooting, and the throwing of Molotov cocktails continued, however, with guardsmen riding "shotgun" on the fire engines. On Saturday evening, an eight o'clock curfew was imposed, and by that time 13,900 National Guardsmen were on duty. The riot ended on Monday, August 16, leaving much of the region looking like the target of an aerial war and white citizens indescribably grateful to Chief of Police William H. Parker.

Among the fundamental causes of the senseless riot were the unavailability of jobs for Negroes, the handicap of their lack of schooling and training, extraordinary transportation problems, Negro resentment and hatred of the police, ineffective Negro leadership, discrimination in almost every field of activity, and a tremendous feeling of frustration among young people, most of whom had never been out of Watts and had seen on television the world they never could attain. During the riot itself, a gleeful love of looting was widely apparent. Looting seemed to be a combination of bargain-hunting and shoplifting.

With the passing of time, the Watts situation seems to be improving. Some progress has been made in job training and job finding. When a Watts Negro gets a good job, he is inclined to move out—his place to be taken by a newcomer. This fact makes it difficult to assess unemployment figures accurately. Police relations have apparently become better. Programs for self-help and self-development are under way, including classes for adult illiterates—classes in English grammar, in Negro history, and in the arts of music, drama, and creative writing. The futility of rioting, with the destruction of neighborhood stores and jobs, has become obvious.

Any recital of racial explosions from the 1850's to the present time presents an unavoidably lopsided picture. Racial tensions have always existed in Los Angeles, but they have not always been highlighted by violence, nor have they had application to every individual or group of individuals. The presenting of violent incidents ignores the day-by-day, year-by-year concern, in Los Angeles, with the difficult and emotional problems arising from or involving de facto segregation. Furthermore, it ignores the brighter phases of good racial relations that over the years have drawn favorable comment from representatives of various races. However, judging from past experience, racial explosions are apt to occur in the future in Los Angeles, but the patterns and modes of expression will not be the same.

7

Cultural "Detonation"

EXCEPT FOR THE FILM INDUSTRY, few of the creative arts in Los Angeles have had far-reaching impact. The local practitioners of painting, sculpture, drama, music, architecture, literature, book design, and other cultural activities have made only a slight impression on the nation and the world. Nevertheless, the rise in Los Angeles during the middle 1960's of glittering centers of the fine arts called attention to the city's vital interest in and intense excitement about the cultural aspects of life.

Ever since California's Spanish and Mexican period, the citizens of Los Angeles have found delight in music and the other arts, expressed in many ways and through different media. The current enthusiasm, however, with embryonic beginnings in the 1920's, largely with the activities of the Los Angeles Philharmonic Orchestra, the Hollywood Bowl (both the products of dedicated Angelenos), and the motion-picture studios, has brought country-wide notice.

During the 1920's, and 1930's, and later decades, Los Angeles was importing musicians, playwrights, and artists to meet the needs of Hollywood. Growing up with them were the potential patrons of the arts: financiers concerned in part with the expansion of business and industrialism that ultimately would transform the city into a super-city. When research scientists, engineers, and technicians began pouring into Southern California during and after World War II, eventually to make it the electronics center of the United States, the tempo of life was accelerated, and imaginative new dimensions were added. Out of the fusion of these combined talents, whether imported or native, grew the emotional stir that has made Los Angeles today a vital and creative city. From this combination came the so-called, and perhaps overemphasized, cultural explosion or detonation of the 1960's.

The history of the fine arts in Los Angeles and in Southern California is interesting, but does not, in a book of this nature, warrant an extensive presentation. However, some mention of the beginnings should be made. Music, in the historic period, began with the Indian choirs and orchestras organized by priests at the neighboring Mission San Gabriel as at other missions. A visitor could report, after listening to a mission choir that "Indian voices accorded harmoniously with the flutes and violins." Through pueblo and rancho days, Southern California is said to have resounded with laughter and song. Every holiday, rodeo, and wedding had its musical accompaniment by violinists, guitarists, and singers. When Pío Pico, California's last Mexican governor, married María Ygnacia Alvarado in 1834, the musical and other festivities in Los Angeles lasted eight days and were attended by nearly everyone of importance from San Diego north. Christmas merrymaking at the Los Angeles plaza in Mexican days included little dramas called *Los Pastores* (the Shepherds), delightful survivors of the medieval miracle plays, with the pueblo furnishing its best amateur actors. The first full band to come to Los Angeles belonged to the forces of Commodore Robert F. Stockton. The band marched in on August 13, 1846. At sunset that day the first concert was given, and, as the lively tunes continued, first the children and then the older people ventured out of their darkened homes. "Ah! that music," commented an old Spanish priest later, "will do more service to the conquest of California than a thousand bayonets." Portrait painters were heavily patronized by prosperous *rancheros* both before and after the conquest. Today the historical museums of Los Angeles and Southern California have scores of ornate portrayals in oil of the *Californios* in all their finery.

Los Angeles had to be satisfied with extremely meager dramatic and musical entertainment in the early American years and at least until the time of the real estate boom of 1887–88. San Francisco, as the metropolis of the West, drew world-famous actors and singers. But "why should they travel to the south five hundred miles in a small and uncomfortable steamer," asked Howard Swan in his comprehensive *Music in the Southwest*, "simply to please a few people in a sleepy and dirty town which had no real theater?"

Some relief from the paucity of dramatic and concert fare came with the opening of the spasmodically conducted Merced Theater in 1870, the Turnverein Hall in 1872, the Grand Opera House in 1884, and Hazard's Pavilion in 1887. The last entertainment house mentioned above could accommodate four thousand persons and witnessed distinguished first nights for grand opera, prize fights, flower festivals, and citrus shows. However, church choirs and various singing and instrumental ensembles provided most of the musical entertainment heard in Los Angeles.

Much of the theatrical and musical development in Los Angeles and Southern California during the first half of the

57

twentieth century can be attributed to the activities of impresario L. E. Behymer, a man deeply interested in music, literature, and the other fine arts. His early associations were with the Burbank Theater, the Los Angeles Theater, Hazard's Pavilion, and the Mason Opera House. Los Angeles was growing, and Behymer was able to bring to his city the most exciting musical personalities of the day. He participated in the founding of the Hollywood Bowl in the twenties and in the establishment there of symphony concerts, although it was Artie Mason Carter, a woman of vision, courage, and driving ability, who should be called the founder of the Bowl and the creator of the famous Symphonies Under the Stars. William A. Clark, Jr., became the first great patron of music in Los Angeles when he established the Los Angeles Philharmonic Orchestra in 1919, with Behymer as its manager, thereby vastly helping the Bowl in its first decade.

The Belasco Theater supplemented the theaters mentioned above by giving Los Angeles pleasing dramatic fare for many years. Oliver Morosco, as a successful stock company manager, provided theatrical entertainment of a high order. Pasadena's Community Playhouse has, since 1916, been greatly responsible for the creation of an interest in drama in the Los Angeles area. Under Gilmor Brown's direction, the Community Playhouse achieved national and international prominence as an innovator of ideas.

Los Angeles, bursting with cultural vitality, has produced three impressive structures in its Civic Center to house musical and theatrical activities during the 1960's. They make up the city's "Music Center for the Performing Arts." In addition, the Los Angeles County Museum of Art, built on Wilshire Boulevard, has made its cultural contribution.

The opening, in 1964, of the Pavilion—now the Dorothy

Chandler Pavilion—the first and most important of the Music Center buildings, evoked this blurb from *Time* magazine: "In a dazzle of diamonds and decolletage, with cinema stars, celebrities and just plain millionaires plentifully on hand, the growing edge of the U.S. population explosion—Los Angeles—welcomed the growing edge of another U.S. explosion—culture."

Among those present for the opening of the Pavilion was Dorothy Buffum Chandler, who conceived the idea for the Music Center and almost singlehandedly raised the money to make the building possible, for whom the Pavilion was named. Another was Welton Becket, the architect, whose building has been described as "a superb musical instrument." Still another was conductor Zubin Mehta, of the Los Angeles Philharmonic Orchestra, who promised the opening-night audience: "This evening we are going to usher in a new era."

The double dedication in April, 1967, of the Mark Taper Forum and the larger Ahmanson Theatre completed the three-theater plan of the Music Center of the Central City. Most of the time, the three theaters perform simultaneously, thus creating a cultural integration that permits a choice of musical and theatrical entertainment. A significant independent organization, the Center Theatre Group, was formed to provide major drama in the Music Center.

The Philharmonic, the Civic Light Opera Association, and the Southern California Symphony–Hollywood Bowl Association moved to the Music Center. This emphasizes the fact that the Los Angeles area has become the home of creative, performing artists: composers, instrumentalists, choreographers, professional actors, chamber music groups, and symphony orchestras. This area is the home of the Pasadena Community Playhouse, the Hollywood Bowl, the

Greek Theatre, the Huntington Hartford Theatre, and various little theater movements. And there are the musical and operatic workshops at the University of California at Los Angeles and the University of Southern California, jazz festivals, and dance concerts.

The Music Center has a broad program intended to encourage and develop the performing arts in Southern California. However, the quality of future Music Center cultural offerings cannot be predicted. Despite its Music Center, Los Angeles is no longer a "theater town."

Opening in April, 1965, the Los Angeles County Museum of Art has made its contribution to a city boiling with artistic activities. Three pavilion-like structures grouped about an open plaza and surrounded by reflecting pools characterize this creation of Architect William Pereira. Facing Wilshire Boulevard, it rests on a yard-thick slab of concrete above the Tar Pits—the famous repository of fossil Pleistocene animal life.

The largest American art gallery to be erected since the completion of the National Gallery in Washington, this museum has the most modern facilities available, but its accumulated works of art, in the words of Katharine Kuh in the *Saturday Review*, "do not add up to a collection." Southern California collectors, and they are numerous, active, and wealthy, gave $11,500,000 to erect the building. These "instant Medicis," to use the magazine *Life*'s phrase, are expected to supply the lack of key masterpieces through a supplemental twelve-million-dollar acquisition fund, the campaign for which was launched early in 1967. Despite this lack, the Museum drew five million visitors in the first two years of its existence. Commenting on the distinguished objects that the Museum does have, on the important private collections in the area, and on the imaginative vigor of

Claire Falkenstein's controversial outdoor fountain a few blocks away from the Museum, Miss Kuh said: "Here [in Los Angeles] art is thrusting out in all directions, and, though these thrusts may sometimes lead to dead ends, the over-all picture is one of bold accomplishment. There is reason to hope that the new museum will become the focus for this city's expanding art life."

Part of the expanding artistic interest finds expression in the one hundred or more commercial galleries in Los Angeles and Beverly Hills. A walk along Los Angeles' La Cienega Boulevard, especially on a Monday evening, will prove that the art business is experiencing a tremendous boom. More paintings are sold in the Los Angeles area, it is said, than in any other American city except New York. Even savings and loan associations sponsor art. The outstanding Lytton Center of the Visual Arts on Sunset Boulevard in Hollywood is an example. Here, Bart Lytton carries out, in part, his program for vigorously supporting contemporary art.

A full story of the current artistic life in the Los Angeles area would detail the activities, collections, and exhibitions of a group of other museums, institutions, colleges, and universities, for many have made valid contributions to the local cultural scene. There is an increasing trend, too, toward outdoor sculpture, appropriate in a mild climate.

As a matter of fact, since the 1850's, the history of painting in the area has been a story of innumerable artists producing and selling works that pleased them and their buyers but that had little, if any, influence on the outside world. Portrait-painting satisfied *ranchero* buyers. Following the impact of the Gold Rush, lithographic drawings of the new urban outgrowths became extremely popular. These lithographs are still delightful records for current viewers and

61

collectors. Local scenery and local activities—including the diminishing rancho life—inspired other artists; many of their paintings and drawings are much sought after by California collectors today. The crumbling missions caused a long line of painters to preserve their romantic outlines in oil and water color. By the middle of the 1870's, Los Angeles was supporting resident artists, large numbers of whom devoted themselves to California landscapes, fields of yellow poppies, or bowls of roses. The town has had many local painters and sculptors, some of whom boasted of training in the studios of Paris, Berlin, London, or New York. In time, the desert and eucalyptus schools developed. Exhibition space, though never adequate, had been available for local and imported shows since the 1890's, when the Ruskin Art Club offered wall space.

By the early 1920's, Los Angeles was becoming acquainted firsthand with abstract paintings. At that time a new era in Southern California art began, an era in which experimental art flourished. Pioneers of this era included Stanton Macdonald-Wright, leader of the Independent Artists of Los Angeles, and Danish-born Knud Merrild, both of whom are internationally known. By the 1930's, Los Angeles was in the current of advanced practices.

In painting, print-making, and sculpture, the contemporary tendencies are bold and imaginative. Artists have their organizations, like the California National Water Color Society and the Women Painters of the West, and reflect a dominant and individual experimentalism.

Today the city of Los Angeles has a Municipal Arts Commission—the governing body of the Municipal Arts Department, which originated in 1903 as a Citizens Committee on Art and which became an official part of city government in 1911. A principal function is approval of any work of art prior to its acceptance by the city and approval of the design of any building or structure on property under city control. In co-operation with the City Recreation and Parks Commission and the Junior League of Los Angeles, the Commission established in Barnsdall Park, in 1967, a Junior Arts Center and Gallery—the first phase of a nine-building cultural complex that is planned for construction. Since the opening in 1954 of the Municipal Art Gallery, designed by Frank Lloyd Wright, located in Barnsdall Park, and made possible by a group of civic-minded art patrons, a series of important exhibitions have been arranged by the Municipal Arts Department, including showings by the better-known southwestern artists. Local artists also present their works in the Tower Gallery in the City Hall and in the annual All City Outdoor Art Festival held each summer in Barnsdall Park.

As a part of the Municipal Arts Department, the Los Angeles Bureau of Music was established in 1944, with the power and the duty to "nurture, promote, sponsor and co-ordinate public interest in music in all its phases and advance the standing of the city as a music center." Chamber music concerts, community sings, Sunday afternoon band concerts, youth voice contests, choral and orchestra concerts, and music therapy are sponsored by the Bureau of Music, together with a Civic Center Orchestra which puts on programs at hospitals, clubs, and elsewhere.

The activities of the Cultural Heritage Board, established by ordinance in 1962, also come within the jurisdiction of the Municipal Arts Department. Admittedly, it began functioning almost too late, for the bulldozer had nearly completed its devastating role. The Board has declared fifty or more buildings and landmarks as historic, cultural monuments for which a permit to demolish, alter, or move may

63

not be obtained without the board's approval. Buildings that have been declared monuments include such significant examples of architecture as the San Fernando Mission, the Leonis Adobe, the Bradbury Building, Frank Lloyd Wright's Hollyhock House in Barnsdall Park, and Simon Rodia's amazing Watts Towers, and natural sites such as Eagle Rock and the thousand-year-old Encino Oak. The Board serves to remind Los Angeles of its cultural heritage by "saving" important survivals of the past that might otherwise be destroyed by surging populations. Its activities have caused other cities to emulate the Board's procedure through similar organizations.

An increasing interest in the preservation of the city's architectural and cultural heritage is seen in the slow but definite development of the Plaza Project, referred to in an earlier chapter, which is resulting in the re-creation of something of Los Angeles' pueblo days. Another evidence of a closely related interest is in the efforts made toward development of the San Fernando Mission–Andrés Pico Historical Center in the San Fernando Valley, also part of the city's vast domain.

In 1965 the Los Angeles County Museum of Art published *A Guide to Architecture in Southern California* which the *New York Times Book Review* declared set "the highest standard yet reached for an architectural guide to any part of the United States." In the preface authors David Gebhard and Robert Winter say that the "City of Los Angeles spreads out like a fungus growth across an immense area. Islands of architectural interest—usually a single building, sometimes a group of buildings—occur almost everywhere in this vast piece of real estate, surrounded by miles of dull repetitive structures." Through maps and photographs, this guide indicates what is interesting, from the architect's point of view, in the Los Angeles area.

Today there are few remnants in Los Angeles of its Mexican past. The flat-roofed, largely single-storied, adobe homes of the pueblo are gone. Anglo-American newcomers in the 1860's, 1870's, and 1880's brought with them the architectural fashions of eastern and middle western cities. These fashions preserved American traditions in Los Angeles and found emphasis in the 1880's when ornate mid-Victorian structures flowered on Los Angeles' Bunker Hill, on Angelino Heights' Carroll Avenue, and in huge and elaborate hostelries. Ultimately the general public, keeping to single-family individual residences, accepted happily the bungalow, then the so-called Spanish-style building, the ranch house, and, with World War II, the proliferating, mass-built tract house. Another type of home, designed for indoor-outdoor living, has been popular and is being copied throughout the country. In public buildings, the Mission style, derived in part from California's Spanish missions and early adobe buildings, was popular between 1905 and 1915. The "Spanish" style in public buildings found its inspiration in the structures of San Diego's Exposition of 1915; one of the last examples in Los Angeles was the Union Station which opened in 1939.

Architects like to call attention to the city's best and worst specimens of architecture—and of the latter, structures both monstrous and infinitely hideous can be found. Attention should be called to the architects who have designed some of the most distinguished buildings: Charles Sumner Greene and Henry Mather Greene, who combined "oriental influence and native sensitivity for wood construction"; Irving Gill, who urged the return to "the straight line, the arch, the cube, and the circle—the mightiest of lines";

65

Frank Lloyd Wright, whose monumental Hollyhock House is now a municipal art center, made possible by the gift of Aline Barnsdall, Los Angeles' first major art patron; Rudolph M. Schindler, who, in the residential field, used a "poetic treatment of form and space"; and Richard J. Neutra, a world figure who approached building design with "refreshing and consistent clarity," his work giving "inspiration to younger men who . . . advanced and made variations upon Neutra's ideas of space and design." Aside from Wright, the architects mentioned were or are permanent Angelenos.

Indicative of the cultural interests of Angelenos are their extensive book-buying habits. As a market for rare books Los Angeles is outranked in the United States, say bookmen, only by New York. Book publishing has expanded remarkably, and currently Los Angeles is active in the field of fine printing. Ward Ritchie, in his "Fine Printing in Southern California," appearing in *A Bookman's View of Los Angeles* (1961), notes that "most of the creative work in the fine book tradition still comes from those printers who began their operations in the thirties." "Eventually," he adds, "there may be another burst of enthusiasm, but in all probability the creative printing of the future will be left to the hobby printers inasmuch as the present tendency throughout this country is the divorce of the printer from the creation of his product." Proving Ritchie's remarks is the continuing and unsurpassed craftsmanship of Saul and Lillian Marks, whose Plantin Press had its beginnings in Los Angeles in 1931. These nationally recognized perfectionists and their work received the accolade of Paul A. Bennett, typographer and critic, in the *Publishers' Weekly* in 1964.

California's productions in the "fine books tradition" are

apt to come out in extremely limited editions. This practice may be scorned by the larger, national publishers, but Angelenos and San Franciscans counter that this practice stimulates and develops a continuing interest in fine printing.

Two Los Angeles social organizations, the Zamorano Club and the Rounce and Coffin Club, with memberships limited to men, are interested in books and printing. The Zamorano Club, corresponding somewhat to Boston's Club of Odd Volumes, New York's Grolier Club, Chicago's Caxton Club, and San Francisco's Roxburghe Club, was organized in Los Angeles in 1928. Named after Agustin V. Zamorano, who in 1834 established the first printing press in California, its members have been and are lawyers, doctors, printers, librarians, editors, writers, and collectors. Some notable bibliographers have been members, among them Henry R. Wagner, who christened the club's quarterly publication *Hoja Volante*—Flying Leaf. Wednesday noon luncheons, followed by visits to antiquarian bookshops, especially Dawson's Bookshop, varied by once-a-month dinner meetings with a speaker, provide a happy outlet for men interested in books, printing, and the pleasures of wine and food. The best known of the club's publications is the *Zamorano Eighty*, presenting a selection of distinguished California books. This volume has been indispensable to the California collector, bookseller, and librarian.

The Rounce and Coffin Club, a merry group who are primarily interested in printing, began sponsoring a "Western Books Exhibition" in 1938—the first of the regional book shows that are now common over most of the United States. Duplicate exhibitions of the best entries of titles printed in the western United States during the preceding year—jury-chosen—are sent out through the area of the contributing printers. Typographical excellence, design, and format—not content—are the bases for selection. These exhibitions are exciting and influential.

The Los Angeles area is littered with writers, few of whom are native Californians, some of them strictly Hollywood importations. Often a famous author, like the late Thomas Mann, may be drawn to Los Angeles because of a Hollywood contract. In such a case, he may not be a native American and may live almost unknown locally, his writing not reflecting his temporary background. Hollywood is not a fly-by-night place, however. Aldous Huxley is an example of the Hollywood writer who stayed to make Los Angeles his home. Year-in and year-out resident writers have their clubs, like The Authors Club and the California Writers Guild.

In 1952, Lawrence Clark Powell, who knows the California scene, admitted, in his *Land of Fiction*: "It is very difficult to write well about this chameleon country . . . . Most of the books until now have been shallow in time. It will probably take generations for the cultural humus to accumulate to a depth on which a great writer can feed. Scouring waves of immigrants make it difficult for anything, save folly, to accumulate for long."

Land of Fiction, bearing the subtitle *Thirty-Two Novels and Stories About Southern California From "Ramona" to "The Loved One,"* covers its subject well up to the date of its appearance. It was issued as a companion volume to J. Gregg Layne's *Books of the Los Angeles District*, published two years earlier in 1950. This work was largely devoted to nonfiction books in the field of regional history. The two little volumes are useful, though they need updating and possibly revamping. Within their scope, however, they describe the best products of writers who have attempted to record or interpret the Los Angeles story. Since their appearance, Los Angeles has been given extensive treatment by writers in fiction and nonfiction. It appears now that some of the most significant work in the widening nonfiction field is being done by college professors in the area.

Los Angeles is well supplied with public and semipublic libraries. The Los Angeles Public Library, with over sixty branches scattered throughout the city's amorphous region, has huge holdings and the largest circulation of books of any library system in America. The general research facilities in the downtown or central library are excellent, and its section devoted to Californiana is extensive. This central library is helpful to other public libraries in the county, whether within Los Angeles or in some other city, for it has an amazing ability to answer any questions tossed its way from the general public and to supply intelligent information on new books.

The Henry E. Huntington Library and Art Gallery, located in San Marino—and therefore within the Los Angeles area—draws scholars from throughout the world to make use of its treasures. As an art gallery, it holds the most important collection of eighteenth century British art in the United States. As a library, it is a "library of libraries." Readers must qualify to gain admittance, and when they do, they have no regrets that such an institution expects to preserve its rarities and books, manuscripts, and works of art through the centuries to come. Another Los Angeles research library that welcomes students and scholars is the richly endowed William Andrews Clark Memorial Library, with its extensive collections of John Dryden and Oscar Wilde materials and its collection of the graphic arts, especially the products of Eric Gill and the contemporary fine printers of Southern California. The Clark Library is administered by the University of California at Los Angeles.

69

Like that of the Huntington Library, its setting is one of tranquil physical beauty.

The Southwest Museum, primarily a library of the Southwest, offers research material on the aborigines of the southwestern United States and on the discovery, exploration, settlement, and development of the same area. Archaeologists, ethnologists, bibliographers, geographers, and historians find their way to the hilltop home of the Southwest Museum. The Los Angeles County Museum of Natural History also draws researchers interested in California history and in science. It is especially rich in its Pleistocene material from the Tar Pits. It has a delightful program of exhibits, activities, and publications.

The cultural contributions of the universities and colleges of the Los Angeles area cannot easily be listed for they are many. The University of California at Los Angeles, the University of Southern California, Loyola, Occidental, Pepperdine, the California State College at Los Angeles, Los Angeles City College, Immaculate Heart, and the University of Judaism, to name only some of the institutions within the physical boundaries of Los Angeles, are centers of scholarly and community endeavors. The University of California at Los Angeles, which spreads massively into all cultural areas, has been set the goal of reaching parity with the University of California at Berkeley in both facilities and in number of students and is zealously racing toward that goal. Within the Los Angeles County area, of course, are many other collegiate and scholarly institutions, among them the Claremont Colleges, which form an embryo Oxford, and the internationally influential California Institute of Technology, located in Pasadena, which is helping to shape America's destiny in space.

There are historical societies and organizations galore in

California—fifty in Los Angeles County alone—and their contributions to culture are obvious, both in the preservation of the area's heritage and in the stimulus to historical research. For the *aficionado* of local history there are city, district, county, regional, and state historical groups with publications, programs, conferences, meetings, and *romerías* spread throughout the entire year. Such a devotee may serve also on a state-appointed commission to preserve landmarks or records of historical events.

The oldest historical organization in Los Angeles is the Historical Society of Southern California, formed in 1883, the year when Angelenos first began to think seriously about their own history. The annual and quarterly publications of this society, issued since 1884, make a fascinating and important library of local and regional history. Contributors have been historians, professional and amateur, pioneers with stories that needed preservation in print, and students whose specific research projects called for publication.

A complete study of publications in local history would reveal constant references to the existence and activities, since the 1850's, of many organizations—social, political, religious, scientific, and patriotic—all of which have made valuable cultural contributions. For example, there are outstanding women's clubs—the Friday Morning Club, the Ruskin Art Club, the Ebell Club, and the Native Daughters of the Golden West—devoted to the cultivation of the fine arts. Churches and religious societies are almost without number. There used to be—perhaps there still is—a Fault Club, a social-scientific, picnicking group of men and women who searched for evidence of earthquakes, past and present. An interesting group is the First Century Families, an informal organization of Angelenos whose families arrived in Los Angeles between 1781 and 1881. Proving that all citizens are not newcomers, the members and guests meet annually—about eight hundred of them—to hear talks on a specific local rancho or other historic spot. There is not room in this little volume to cover all of these organizations, and I do not have the temerity or the knowledge to attempt the feat.

If all this proliferation of activities and interests makes for a cultural "detonation" or "explosion" in Los Angeles, so be it. At least there is a fury of movement.

8

Spanish-Mexican Heritage

TODAY, LOOKING AT the endless subdivisions sprawling over the valleys and hills of Los Angeles, through and over which freeways flow with nearly four million automobiles, it is hard to conceive of the great ranchos—Spanish and Mexican—devoted to raising cattle and a feudal way of life which once dotted the area. It is hard to believe—yet also true—that relics of the rancho days are numerous and may still be visited and enjoyed. The bulldozer has not destroyed everything, and both visitor and resident Angeleno may sample something of the flavor of the past. Even the names of old ranchos and old families, surviving in localities and streets, are sweet to the ear.

Picture the area in the year 1845, under the Mexican regime, when the pueblo of Los Angeles was the capital of Alta California—the hub of the ranchos of the southland, and the southern social, shopping, and political center. From this small town of one-story flat-roofed adobe houses and shops, clustered about a dusty plaza, fanned a half dozen roads. These roads followed the curves and dips of the rolling landscape to and through the encircling ranchos. They provided access to the port of San Pedro, where hides could be traded for necessities or for luxury items from New England and China, and to the lively presidio towns of Santa Barbara on the north and San Diego on the south.

Today these routes have straightened themselves into broad highways or have been supplemented or superseded by freeways—still devoted, as in rancho days, to the purposes of communication, business, and pleasure. Their network overlays the old ranchos and makes it possible to travel quickly from downtown Los Angeles to outlying areas which were once reached only by horseback or by ox-drawn *carretas*. These routes, if traced carefully, lead to interesting survivals of Spanish-Mexican days—thick-walled adobe-brick homes from which *rancheros* once directed the activities of their ranchos, thousands of acres in extent. Some of these structures bear the numbers of state-registered landmarks, and may be visited freely. Others are privately owned and may only be looked at by passers-by, who find them as interesting as the homes of film personalities.

The starting point for the first excursion into rancho days is logically the old Los Angeles plaza itself. It can be reached by a short drive north on Main Street in the downtown section, continuing for about a block beyond the intersecting, and undercutting Hollywood–Santa Ana Freeway. Here is the plaza of rancho days, dominated now as always by the church that served the *rancheros* and townsmen. Today it serves people in the neighboring area and part of Los Angeles' huge Mexican-American population. The plaza is now owned by the state. It is part of a larger area acquired under a master plan to preserve and re-create a sampling of the founding, rancho, and pueblo days of Los Angeles.

About this plaza grew the pueblo through Spanish, Mexican, and early American administrations. On the roads leading to it galloped *rancheros* who came to town to arrange cattle deals, to see what was new in saddles, to visit the liquor shops, to play a little monte in a gambling house, or perhaps to see a horse race or bullfight. They called on friends and occasionally on the priest, especially if a baptism, wedding, or burial was being arranged. The women of the ranchos, arriving in canopied *carretas*, stopped in town houses—their own or those of friends. They shopped for bargains in furniture from New England, shawls from China, or pointed shoes from Mazatlán. They and their husbands or brothers attended balls where guitarists, violinists, and singers furnished music for dancing the *bamba*, *contradanza*, the *fandango*, and the *jota*. Other members of a rancho's feudal organization also visited the pueblo and the plaza for business or fun. All found the pueblo entrancing.

Rancho days did not end with the take-over by the United States in 1846–48; the plaza saw its best days in the prosperous early 1850's when cattle brought their highest prices. At that time one-story town houses acquired second stories and four-poster beds. Their owners and their horses wore fancy outfits, shops bulged with luxuries, and fiestas and religious ceremonies became more elaborate. Bullfighting had already been moved to a ring some distance away, but cockfighting was still a plaza feature. Today, unfortunately, the town houses that once faced the plaza—those owned by the Carrillos, the Lugos, the del Valles, Judge Olvera, and others—are all gone. What is left is the church, the Pico House (early-day hotel), and an old firehouse—receiving the attention of preservers and restorers, with other buildings farther away scheduled for ultimate reactivation.

One surviving town house, formerly belonging to the Avila family, can be visited on Olvera Street, a one-block-long lane leading north from the middle of the plaza. Now furnished in the manner and spirit of rancho days, the thick-walled Avila House, dating from possibily 1818 and much smaller now than it once was, invites visitors, for a twenty-five-cent fee, to walk through its cool interior and interesting rooms. The patio in the rear has been developed into a charming garden dominated by trees and vines. This house symbolizes and stimulates the reactivation of the whole plaza area.

The transformation of Olvera Street, in the late 1920's and early 1930's, into a "picturesque Mexican market place" followed the "save the Avila House" movement. Transformed from a slum and crime center, it has become a gay, amusing, and, to children at least, enchanting thoroughfare. This street of spicy smells, gaily colored booths, shops, restaurants, and wandering musicians supports three to four hundred Mexican-American families and draws at least two million visitors a year. While not pretending to be a restoration from the days of the ranchos, Olvera Street is genuine, offering to those who throng its length in the evenings many of the foods, the leather and silver work, the basketry, the Mexican shoes, the strings of gourds, the toys, the *piñatas*, the cactus candy, the jumping beans, and the whatnots of villages below the border.

A trip through Pasadena and the San Gabriel Valley to the Los Angeles State and County Arboretum is definitely an excursion into rancho country. The Pasadena Freeway (Highway 66) leads to Colorado Boulevard, which takes one east across Rancho San Pascual, now the city of Pasadena, and into Rancho Santa Anita—through areas once grazed by the sheep and cattle of Mission San Gabriel and later by the stock of the *rancheros*.

The arboretum, occupying a fragment (127 acres) of the

76

13,000-acre Mexican grant of Santa Anita, is reached by leaving Highway 66 at Baldwin Avenue, the western boundary of the famous Santa Anita Race Track. Inside the arboretum grounds, a "jeep train" takes the visitor quickly through delightful plantings to the Hugo Reid Adobe. This is located on the edge of a five-acre lagoon surrounded by tropical trees and with a view of blue, distant mountains. Low-lying, whitewashed, and flat-roofed, the adobe, restored and reconstructed by the state, is typical of the small, ranch-style house built in Southern California in the 1840's, the kind of structure that usually expanded as the family increased in number. It was used by Reid, "the Scotch *paisano*," first owner of the rancho. From this three-room house he or his foreman (*mayordomo*) ran the cattle ranch of Santa Anita. A larger home nearer Mission San Gabriel, no longer in existence, provided space for his family and his hospitality.

A glimpse through the latticed windows into the rooms of the Reid Adobe reveals the hard-packed, earthen floors and the ceilings of reed tied with rawhide strips and waterproofed by tar brought from La Brea Tar Pits eight miles west of the pueblo. Its furnishings are the simple tables, chairs, beds, and miscellaneous items typical of the 1840's.

Before taking a jeep back to the arboretum entrance, visitors usually like to feed the ducks and peacocks waddling or strutting at the lagoon's edge. The peacocks are descendants of the peacocks imported by a later owner and famous horseman, Lucky Baldwin, who struck it rich in Nevada's Comstock Lode and bought Santa Anita in 1875. Across the lagoon, behind the palms, is Baldwin's pleasure pavilion, a gingerbread Victorian structure, called, oddly, "The Queen Anne Cottage," where he entertained his lady friends.

77

Highway 66 takes one swiftly past the modern Santa Anita Race Track, through the city of Arcadia, and over five old Mexican ranchos that have become nine cities. When the visitor reaches Pomona, which arose on Rancho San José, he turns right on Garey Avenue. A few blocks farther, at 491 East Cucamonga (Arrow Highway), is the charming thirteen-room Adobe de Palomares, owned by the city of Pomona and leased and run for the benefit of the visiting public by the Historical Society of Pomona Valley.

From this T-shaped casa, with a front patio and a family patio, Don Ygnacio Palomares directed the members of his family and his Indian *vaqueros* and helpers in all the activities that involved a large part of the Pomona (San José) Valley when it was a huge cattle ranch. The first room entered is the little store (*tienda*) which catered to the procession of early-day travelers who came, by horseback, wagon, or stagecoach, along the old San Bernardino road. Aside from this room and another devoted to exhibits in glass cases, the house is maintained as it was before Don Ygnacio's death in 1864.

When visitors step into a bedroom—literally the master's bedroom—they are told that with the dawn Don Ygnacio raised his voice in a hymn, or *alabado*, to be joined in sleepily or joyously by the rest of his family. When dressed, they hastened to the living room (*sala*) where Don Ygnacio led in morning prayers. Breakfast over, the family scattered to the tasks of the day, the men to spend the greater part of the time in the saddle, the women to perform household duties. When wash day came, the daughters made it a picnic. They and their Indian girls took lunches and the piles of saved-up clothes and sheets and, climbing into an ox-drawn *carreta*, rode across the field to a spring and a stream. Here they scrubbed the clothes, spread them out on the grass and bushes to dry, and then plunged into the water themselves.

In the large, cool *sala*, a dancing party lasting a week took place when a son, Manuel Palomares, married Carmelita Rubidoux of the neighboring Rancho Jurupa. Two groups of musicians were employed, so that one could sleep while the other played. When the priest from San Gabriel called, he was given a guest bedroom adjoining the *sala* and was told to use one end of the *sala* as a chapel. All the rooms in Casa de Palomares are furnished with rancho-period pieces, and the patios and grounds are planted as they were in the 1860's. There are languid peppers, along with such fruit trees as figs, walnuts, and pomegranates, a huge grapevine from the mission stock, and roses of Castile. A cactus fence in the rear formerly kept wandering cattle from peering in the windows. An outdoor beehive oven, along with the small inside kitchen, provided good eating for many people. An old-time well and an adobe blacksmith shop are nearby. All are there to remind the visitor of a way of life devoted primarily to the raising of long-horned cattle for the purpose of transforming them into dried beef and marketable hides and tallow.

Leaving the casa, a shortcut takes the visitor to the modern San Bernardino Freeway and a quick ride back to Los Angeles.

The rancho-day homes surviving in Southern California are many and varied, in spite of the proliferation of subdivisions and the devastating work of the bulldozer. Possibly the largest home in the Los Angeles area is the stately, thick-walled Casa de Rancho Los Cerritos at 4600 Virginia Road, Long Beach—close to the Virginia Country Club. The builder was Don Juan Temple, owner of the 27,000-acre Rancho Los Cerritos ("the little hills"), which with the adjoining Rancho Los Alamitos ("the little cotton-woods"), included all of present-day Long Beach. From the huge ranch house, Don Juan governed the domain upon which he pastured 15,000 cattle, 7,000 sheep, and 3,000 horses. To make Los Cerritos self-sustaining, Temple enlisted people of special skills—harness-makers, tanners, wool-combers, blacksmiths, and carpenters—and a retinue of Indian *vaqueros* and servants. The foundations of the casa, which he built in 1844, were bricks brought around the Horn. The beams and floors were of hand-hewn redwood obtained from forests near Monterey. Los Cerritos and Los Alamitos were friendly rivals. Annually there was horse racing between the two ranchos, the race extending from El Cerrito (Signal Hill) straight to the beach. Important features of life on both ranchos, as on all ranchos, were the rodeos—when cattle and horses were periodically rounded up, segregated, and branded. A "judge of the plains," appointed by the pueblo council, decided disputes over ownership. Rodeos, incidentally, were social affairs enlivened by horse racing, bullfights, feasting, and dancing. Owned today by the city of Long Beach, Casa de Rancho Los Cerritos is maintained by the Long Beach Public Library. A trip through the many rooms of its cool interior is a pleasure and an education.

Also in the Long Beach area is the equally fascinating Rancho Los Alamitos. What remains is a seven-and-one-half-acre parcel still owned by the Bixby family of rancho fame. Included there is one of the most charming houses in the state. It dates from the Spanish period, possibly from the year 1806. Surrounding this home is a garden that delights the eye. It is probable that the city of Long Beach may acquire this place, as it did Casa de Rancho Los Cerritos. The property was left in trust to the children of the rancho's last owner, Fred H. Bixby.

The Pico Mansion, in the Whittier area, is certainly worth visiting. It was the home of the last Mexican governor of Alta California, Pío Pico, a man who loved gaming, horse races, and hospitality. He called it, affectionately, "El Ranchito," because the rancho was so small—only nine thousand acres.

San Fernando Valley has its relics of rancho days, not only the Mission of San Fernando itself but several houses that belonged to well-known *rancheros*. In the Encino area is the wide adobe ranch house that was a favorite stopping place for *Californios* traveling from the pueblo to the presidio of Santa Barbara. Its owner was Don Vicente de la Osa. When hard times hit Don Vicente, he put a notice in the Los Angeles *Star* requesting visitors to "please bring money." Near the Mission itself is the Andrés Pico (or Romulo Pico) house, originally used by Eulogio de Celis, first owner of the fabulous Rancho Ex-Mission de San Fernando with its 116,000 acres. In Calabasas is the Miguel Leonis Adobe, a pleasant example of an early California home, a two-story building with white walls and red roofs. Both the Andrés Pico and the Miguel Leonis adobes were saved from destruction through the efforts of the Cultural Heritage Board and various dedicated citizens. The Leonis house was scheduled to give way to a shopping center, but today it is open to the public and is a delight to visitors.

In the immediate Los Angeles area are a number of privately owned homes that date from rancho days. Such are the surviving adobes of the great cattle-owning family of Don Antonio María Lugo, who symbolized the California *ranchero*, riding erect in his saddle even to old age and carrying a Spanish-style sword at his side. On the grounds of the Farmer's Market is the former adobe home of Don Antonio Rocha, first owner of Rancho La Brea. It exists today in restored form and is privately owned and occupied. Don Antonio's great-granddaughter, Mrs. Senaida Sullivan, a member of the Cultural Heritage Board, lives in another adobe home built in 1865 and located on the former Rancho Rincon de los Bueyes.

Many of the favorite visiting places of tourists in the Los Angeles area are located on land which once belonged to great ranchos. Marineland is on Rancho Los Palos Verdes; Disneyland is on Rancho San Juan Cajon de Santa Ana; the Hollywood Bowl and the new Los Angeles Museum of Art are on Rancho La Brea.

To get the full flavor of the pastoral era and to become thoroughly aware of the Angeleno's cultural heritage, the tourist should visit San Diego and Santa Barbara. These former presidio towns are fully conscious of their inheritance from Spain and Mexico.

Anyone wishing a pleasant short cut to the past without traveling should visit the Casa de Adobe, immediately below the Southwest Museum at 4605 North Figueroa Street in Los Angeles. Here one gets the story of rancho living in capsule form. The casa, owned by the Southwest Museum, is a composite built to perpetuate authentically the best of the California rancho period. It was modeled after a San Diego County ranch house, that on Rancho Guajome. That house had remained intact since the pastoral era, a thick-walled, red-tiled, twenty-room residence built in four long wings and opening upon a landscaped patio and garden. It was not merely a house, it was a complete economic unit sufficient for operating a cattle ranch and taking care of all the needs of the owner and his Indian

82

servants in a feudal society. Even a jail and a chapel were included.

The Casa de Adobe today inspires architects attempting to simulate an early California type of home. Also, it is the delight of visitors, children and adults, who swarm through the corridors and learn firsthand how Californians of the rancho period warmed their rooms, how they did their cooking, what sort of dishes they used, what their beds were like, how they took baths, and what kind of chapels they used for worship. In one year, sixty schools may send several thousand pupils through the casa. Classes in adult education and teacher groups are also special guests. Bluebirds, Brownies, Boy Scouts, and Cub Scouts often take the tour.

Traditional with the casa have been the May fiesta of the Holy Cross and the December Posadas, occasions when the spirit of early California finds happy expression. At both affairs, highlights of the year in rancho days, religious ceremonial blends joyfully with fun-making.

At the May fiesta, singing and dancing finally take over completely. With violins and guitars providing the music, costumed couples dominate the temporary stage set up in the patio. The couples have included the Dancing Lugos, descendants of the famous *ranchero* Antonio María Lugo, who keep up the dances of their ancestors; and the Ruiz California Dancers, with their authentic old-time group dances. They provide fast steps, swirling skirts, clapping hands, stamping feet, shouts, the sound of castanets, and the singing of amorous verses.

The ceremony of Las Posadas—with its fundamental appeal to everybody—is held on a Sunday evening close to Christmas. Braziers in the patio, holding burning coals, provide warmth and flickering light. Enacted by members of Los Californios, the crowd of children and adults join in the procession behind Joseph and Mary, who are seeking lodging. Each person carries a lighted candle. All sing the stately, old music of Las Posadas. Rebuffed at three stops, Joseph and Mary and those who follow finally enter the chapel of the casa, arranged with a traditional nativity setting, where lodging for the night has been granted. The program ends with lively music from strolling musicians and with especial fun for the children. The gay, gift-filled *piñata* is dangled before blindfolded children, one child at a time. Striking about with a long stick, some lucky child finally breaks open the bag, and a scramble for gifts follows. Then *cascarones* are passed about—and who does not get a confetti-filled egg cracked on his head?

9

Expanding Empire of a Newspaper

So POTENT AND DOMINANT is the influence of the Los Angeles *Times* throughout its empire that no study of Los Angeles is complete without an attempt to portray this colossus.

I have read and watched this newspaper since the time it was directed by the fire-eating, labor-union-hating General Harrison Gray Otis. And beginning in 1960, I have watched a revitalization, transformation, and expansion by the general's great-grandson, Otis Chandler.

In the pre-6:00 A.M. weekday dawn, a thick five-, six-, or seven-part bundle is plumped on my driveway and on the driveways of most Angelenos. On Sunday comes a monstrous, cylindrical package containing more parts, sections, and magazines than I can easily count. This bundle or package is the Los Angeles *Times*.

Today the *Times* seems to be excited about the whole world and to be falling over backwards in its attempt at objective reporting. Yesterday—that is, in the General's day—it was concerned primarily with the local scene and was one of the most biased and vituperative journals in existence. In that early day, it dealt brutally with its en-

85

emies. For example, it normally referred to labor-union members as "sluggers," "rowdies," "bullies," "gas-pipe ruffians," "brutes," "roughnecks," "anarchists," "blather-skites," "pinheads," and "skunks." Today it has a labor editor who could not be politer in writing about the doings and sayings of labor leaders.

When the *Times* endorses a candidate today, he is apt to wonder from then on why he must read such bad news about himself in that supposedly friendly journal. So Richard Nixon, Barry Goldwater, and Ronald Reagan—all of whom belatedly received the backing of the *Times* must have wondered.

When the *Times* presents an editorial perhaps praising or favorably analyzing some proposal or activity of the President of the United States or of the mayor of Los Angeles, that editorial may be opposed by Paul Conrad's cartoon, which, dominating the same page on the same day, is quite likely to hold the President or the mayor up to savage ridicule. Such "objectivity" is either a sign of editorial maturity or the mark of editorial irresponsibility. The fine-print disclaimer, that "the *Times*' official position on issues is expressed only in the two columns below," does not offset the cartoon—the heart of the page. Other cartoonists and a whole menagerie of columnists, presenting liberal, moderate, or conservative points of view, occupy the following pages. Thus the *Times* does succeed in attaining genuine objectivity.

Today if the *Times* is attacked at a public meeting or in a letter directed to the *Times* or in a lawsuit against the *Times* or in a news story, the attack is given full and impartial publicity—even though members of the Chandler family are involved. The *Times* is usually slow in taking a stand on a public issue, but when it does, a staff member of the newspaper may take an opposing position. When the *Times* at the last minute opposed a library bond issue, the book editor, Robert Kirsch, at the same time wrote strongly in favor of the proposition.

The "new," "objective" *Times* has hardly been in the field long enough for its influence on voters to be assessed. In earlier days a recommendation from the *Times* was apt to be the deciding factor among Angeleno voters. They simply voted "no" whenever the paper said to vote "yes."

According to the *Wall Street Journal*, Otis Chandler says: "We're still a Republican newspaper, but we've tried to divorce our editorial news from our news reporting. We think that readers, with only two metropolitan newspapers in Los Angeles—and other media to turn to, such as television and magazines—are demanding a better balance in the presentation of news."

With the death, in 1962, of the afternoon *Mirror* and the morning *Examiner*, the *Times'* only surviving metropolitan competitor became the afternoon, Hearst-owned *Herald-Examiner*. In addition, there are various suburban competitors in the Los Angeles area—some of them small publications located in incorporated cities within the county, others, like the *Valley Times*, widely read in the teeming San Fernando Valley. To meet this suburban situation, the Los Angeles *Times* issues a special "zone section," which covers the news of a particular section and is included in the newspaper that is delivered to subscribers living in that section.

To cover national and world news, the *Times* greatly expanded its domestic and foreign bureaus. It corraled Pulitzer Prize winners and raided the staffs of New York newspapers and national magazines for additional reporters. It recruited newsmen based in Los Angeles but ready to fly anywhere to cover major stories. It has legal, medical, labor, science, society, entertainment, education, and urban affairs editors, as well as a staff jazz critic.

The great turnabout in *Times* policies and direction came in 1960 when Otis Chandler, then thirty-three, succeeded his father, Norman Chandler, as publisher. Influential in the change was Dorothy Buffum Chandler, Norman's wife and Otis' mother. This woman of charm, ability, and force took upon herself the public relations and promotional phases of the business. Under Otis Chandler, a complete editorial overhaul took place.

It is true that the *Times*, under both Norman Chandler and Norman's father, Harry Chandler, who married General Otis' daughter, had largely discarded "fire-eating journalism" and had become a temperate and financially solid newspaper. But now, under young Otis—and stimulated and aided by a strong staff—the *Times* received a fantastic infusion of new ideas and new blood.

An impetus in the rapid transformation of the *Times* was provided when the *New York Times* attempted to establish a western edition to provide the West Coast with an extensive coverage of national and international news. After long planning, it began distribution in October, 1962, and attained a circulation of one hundred thousand. Then it began to fail, suffering financial loss for sixteen months, and finally folding in January, 1964. The failure can be accounted for by the fact that the Los Angeles *Times*, rising to the challenge, was giving readers what they wanted. This victory gave it the incentive to expand in all directions.

Editorial policy is shaped by Otis Chandler and a group of editors who meet daily. They include Nick B. Williams, editor, and James Bassett, director of the editorial pages.

Major decisions may call for consultation with Norman Chandler.

Norman Chandler, chairman and chief executive of the Times Mirror Company, the parent organization, is concerned with expanding the Times-Mirror empire into the field of information and education. The company has acquired a variety of businesses, including a string of publishing houses such as the World Publishing Company and the New American Library, together with a bindery. It has a division, the Times Mirror Press, which prints southwestern telephone directories. The Times Mirror Company also owns a plywood company, several newspapers, and many other properties. With the Los Angeles *Times* as its base, the parent company has made diversification pay enormous profits.

In a few months Franklin D. Murphy, now chancellor of U.C.L.A., is scheduled to succeed Norman Chandler as chairman and chief executive officer of the Times Mirror Company. Norman Chandler is to become chairman of the corporation's Executive Committee. Albert V. Casey is to continue as its president. Otis Chandler is to remain as publisher of the *Times* and to become vice-chairman of the Times Mirror Company's board.

Among the reasons given for the Los Angeles *Times'* current success have been the end of morning competition and the demise of the *New York Times'* efforts to establish a western foothold, its good management in a fast-growing area, its ability to get newsprint cheaper than most papers, and its non-union status. To these patent reasons might be added the Chandler family's probably intense desire to change the image created by the pugnacious and uncompromising General Otis who had acquired control of the newspaper in 1886.

A look at the incredible *Times* of yesterday will help one to understand the "great leap forward" the *Times* has made. Under General Otis' direction, the *Times* was the very personal expression of one man's opinion. If the General liked a man, he liked him on every page. If he disliked or hated him, there was venom in every mention of that man in the *Times*. Otis, a veteran of fifteen Civil War battles, remained a warrior for the rest of his life. And he fought without giving quarter. He even named his home The Bivouac, and his personal stationery bore that label. The Times Building itself resembled a medieval fortress, adorned by an eagle with outspread wings.

The personal journalism exhibited by the *Times* is evident in the following story. In 1903 the *Times* handled the news of the approaching nuptials of Wallace Hardison, a prominent oil man, a long-time enemy of Otis, and the owner of the competing *Los Angeles Herald*. The five-line heading that preceded the story, apparently coming from Kansas, declared:

KANSAS SINGER TO MARRY HARDUPSON
TELEGRAPH BRINGS NEWS THAT HE IS WEALTHY
WONDER IF THE BRIDE ELECT REALLY THINKS SO
NUPTIALS SET FOR APRIL
AND THE TROUBLES OF MARY BELLE WILL THEN BEGIN

Rough and ready Wallace Hardison did not like this reportage. He immediately "went for" General Otis. He found Otis in the Los Angeles Theater, occupying a box seat and enjoying the matinee of *The Heart of Maryland*. Hardison assaulted Otis then and there, and Otis had to be rescued by the police.

The *Times* was the big Southern California newspaper in General Otis' day. It could afford to ignore—for a time—

the almost continual sniping from the small-town newspapers in the area. Then, like a St. Bernard turning finally to
stop the nagging nuisance of a snapping fox terrier, the
Times would dispatch star reporter Harry Carr to the of-
fending town—in one case to Riverside to give the full
treatment to Editor E. P. Clarke of the *Riverside Daily
Press*. Under "Great Editors I Have Met," Carr presented
an amusing prose portrayal of the angular, "frost-bitten"
Clarke, who rode to his tasks on a bicycle, sang lustily in the
Methodist choir, etc. The Clarke story was one of a series.

General Otis' great crusade was against labor unions, and
to him it was a "holy war." Year in and year out he fought
to maintain the open shop in Los Angeles and to make his
town the citadel of "industrial freedom." He successfully
kept unionism out of Los Angeles, and he helped local
industrialists win the strikes that came their way. By 1910,
however, "the labor situation in Los Angeles had begun to
assume the ugly characteristics of a class war," to quote historian Robert G. Cleland. A series of strikes involving many
trades pointed up the tenseness of the situation. The city
council passed an anti-picketing ordinance which was challenged by strikers; there were many arrests. San Francisco
was then backing the Los Angeles strikes, for the northern
city feared the open shop would be brought there unless
equalization of wages and working conditions through un-
ionization were achieved in Los Angeles.

At this climactic period, the extremist leaders of the
International Association of Bridge and Structural Iron
Workers made Los Angeles their target. For over three
years they had directed, from Indianapolis, a dynamite
campaign against steel construction projects erected by
non-union labor. They had caused nearly one hundred explosions through time-bombs placed by experienced sabo-

91

teurs. The secretary of the ironworkers' association, John J. McNamara, chose the buildings to be destroyed and assigned the men to carry out the dynamiting jobs. Several Los Angeles structures were marked for destruction, but naturally the Times Building was the highest on the list, for Otis and his newspaper symbolized everything the labor leaders hated.

On the night of September 30, 1910, James B. McNamara, brother of John, deposited a suitcase in "Ink Alley" behind the Times Building. The suitcase contained a time-bomb set to go off at 1:00 A.M. It actually went off at 1:07 A.M. In moments the whole building was ablaze, and the men trapped inside—twenty *Times* employees—died in the fire.

The dynamiting of the *Times* became a national affair in April, 1911. In that month the two McNamara brothers and Ortie McManigal, a saboteur whose confession implicated the McNamaras and revealed the national dynamiting conspiracy, were rushed from Indianapolis, turned over to California officials, placed in the Los Angeles County Jail, and charged with the crime. At that time the public knew nothing of the dynamiting program directed by the leaders of the International Association of Bridge and Structural Iron Workers or of the amazing adventures in sleuthing by William J. Burns detectives which preceded the arrests.

The whole of organized labor was aghast. The somewhat "informal" arrests were called "kidnaping," and the labor unions of America rushed to the McNamaras' defense. They believed the McNamaras were being railroaded to the gallows on manufactured evidence. A defense fund was started—the money to come from contributions made by working men of the United States and labor sympathizers.

Clarence Darrow, considered the country's best criminal lawyer and a defender of working men, was persuaded by Samuel Gompers, president of the American Federation of Labor, to defend the prisoners. A retainer fee of $50,000 and an expense account of $200,000 or more were given him.

The charge against James B. McNamara was that of dynamiting the Los Angeles Times Building. That against John J. McNamara was of dynamiting the Llewellyn Iron Works in Los Angeles—a follow-up job directed by him and carried out by McManigal as a Christmas Eve present.

Between the jailing of the McNamaras in April, 1911, and the beginning of the trial in October, the national uproar over the case continued at an ever increasing tempo. Throughout the United States, May Day, 1911, was "McNamara Day." Country-wide demonstrations were held. In Los Angeles, twenty thousand banner-carrying, shouting men marched by the Temple Street Jail where the McNamaras were confined.

Union leaders early developed the theory that escaping gas, rather than dynamite, was responsible for the explosion. Extremists believed that Otis himself had plotted the destruction of his own building. A statement issued on October 26, 1910, by the California State Federation of Labor Committee carried this heading: "Otis Is the Criminal." It then devoted four newspaper-sized pages to the story of Otis and his alleged nefarious activities. By the time the case against the McNamaras came to trial in Los Angeles, on October 11, it was an international *cause célèbre*.

A climactic event took place on December 1, 1911, upon the convening of Judge Bordwell's court. Ordinarily court met in the morning, but on this day, at the request of District Attorney Fredericks, it was adjourned until afternoon. "Grave matters," Fredericks explained, had to be considered. Newsmen were puzzled.

It all happened very quickly and as planned. Both defendants pleaded guilty.

The results of this double confession were devastating, locally and nationally. In Los Angeles, the gutters were littered with McNamara buttons, while at the Labor Temple on Maple Avenue crowds talked of necktie parties for the McNamaras and Darrow. Election day—December 5—happened to be the day Judge Bordwell sentenced James B. to life and John to fifteen years, both in San Quentin. At the polls, Job Harriman, pro-McNamara Socialist leader and candidate for mayor, was overwhelmed in defeat. Throughout the country responsible labor leaders were amazed, sorrowful, and angry. For organized labor the affair resulted in a twenty-five-year setback and gave the Socialist party a blow from which it has never recovered.

Despite the dynamiting affair, Otis continued his personal style of journalism, and the outspoken *Times* continued to defend itself in lawsuits. One of the best publicized was the action brought in 1915 by Joseph Scott against the Times Mirror Company for civil libel.

Scott had been a member of the defense counsel representing the McNamara brothers. This did not endear him to the *Times*, which showed its hostility on many occasions. Scott had a file of derogatory clippings. The culminating clipping was an article which strongly implied that Scott, who was attorney for a wealthy Pasadena woman who was suing for divorce, was taking advantage of the woman. The jury found the newspaper guilty, and Scott was awarded $7,500 compensatory damages and $30,000 punitive damages. The California Supreme Court affirmed the judgment.

A check for $47,549.71—including costs of appeal—was written by the Times Mirror Company in favor of Joseph Scott. For years afterwards an enlarged, framed photograph of that check hung in Scott's office. When I called on Scott, he took me to the picture, pointed it out, and told me how he taught the *Times* the law of libel. By that time he had become a good friend of the newspaper and its owners.

Two years after the dynamiting, a new *Times* building occupied the site at First and Broadway in Los Angeles. Harry Chandler, Otis' son-in-law and a man with good financial sense, took over as publisher in 1917, upon the death of General Otis. The old-fashioned, vituperative spirit —which makes pioneering journalism so interesting in retrospect—mostly died with Otis. The *Times* entered into an expansive phase in 1935 when it occupied a complete and modern newspaper plant at First and Spring streets, a building of structural beauty. Norman Chandler, son of Harry, became the *Times* publisher in 1945. Today, under the direction of Norman's tall, athletic son, Otis, the tremendous expansion of the paper and its change in editorial approach cause national comment.

As a daily reader of the Los Angeles *Times*, I have my own reactions to this newspaper and its coverage. They do not comprise a Gallup Poll but may serve to indicate the contents and coverage of this newspaper.

My newspapers are read religiously—the *Times* in the early morning, the *Wall Street Journal* in mid-morning, for it comes by mail, and the *Herald-Examiner* in the early evening. Before breakfast I glance over page one of the *Times*. During breakfast, with my wife present, I furtively look at a page or two, avoiding outright discourtesy. If I am rather silent during this meal, it is because page one already has dominated and depressed me with the sad import of most

95

of its foreign and national news. After breakfast I settle down in an easy chair and really read the *Times* from cover to cover.

In reading a typical Monday morning *Times*, I first pick up a thirty-page Part One. The first page of that section is almost exclusively concerned with foreign news, although there is room for a small amount of national news. A local event, to be worthy of that page, apparently has to be significant, sensational, or of universal human interest. There is a brief and convenient feature index to all the newspaper's parts, together with a brief weather, and smog, forecast. Naturally, I read the first page rather carefully. The second page I skim through, for it is a summary of the news of the day—world, nation, state, southland, metropolitan, business, and sports. Important local news, like the Emmy Awards, gets splashy treatment on the third page. Thereafter, Part One of the *Times* is largely devoted to national and international events. I note, partly read, and at least skim through a great variety of dispatches from Gettysburg, Boston, Cape Kennedy, Paris, Washington, Israel, Atlanta, New Orleans, Brazil, Cairo, and New York. One column is devoted to the status of major bills in Congress. Many columns are devoted to carry-overs from stories started on the first and third pages. A dog show in Pasadena in which a miniature poodle is the winner will be covered. There is an obituary page with brief stories about prominent persons who have died. Finally, there is a "Southland" page.

To the other five or six parts of the *Times*, I give quite full attention. Part Two, the metropolitan section, carries local news and the *Times*' own editorials, together with the work of syndicated columnists and certain *Times* staff men. I always read the *Times* editorials, but I am disappointed when they do not show the expertness displayed in the *Wall*

Street Journal. The *Times* owners, or board of directors, I am sure, would be far happier if they did not have to present personal editorial opinion or endorse candidates.

Scattered through the other parts are feature sections devoted to art, book reviews, business and finance, City Hall, entertainment, motion pictures, music, sports, television and radio, comics, churches, vital records, and a detailed weather report.

In these sections, I have my favorite writers. Among them are Jack Smith, who successfully talks about himself and his family; Charles Champlin, the amusing entertainment editor; Bill Henry, the *Times'* own Washington commentator, forever good at quick and cogent analysis; Jim Murray, who is so good on sports that he ought to be writing in other realms, which he does; Robert Kirsch, an avaricious reader and knowledgeable book editor; Ray Hebert, the urban affairs editor who writes adroitly about city planning; Matt Weinstock, who always has an amusing localism or two; the current real estate editor, who knows his real estate; Maggie Savoy, society editor, who writes glamorously of all the parties I am not invited to; Art Seidenbaum, who frequently presents an intriguing point of view; and the various contributors who write for the business and finance section.

10

Myth-Making

THE LOS ANGELES AREA, beset always by waves of new-comers, has produced its full share of myths. Its people prefer to accept and retell stories which seem good enough to be true, even if they are not.

Long before there was a Los Angeles and before California was looked upon by the navigator Juan Cabrillo, the whole region was shrouded in clouds of myth. As early as 1510, California, as yet unseen by white men, was reputed to be an island inhabited by black, passionate Amazons. The island part of this myth long persevered, but, needless to say, the Amazonian element was short lived.

Los Angeles lies on the site of the prehistoric Shoshonean village of Yang-na. The myth that the village was located at or near the southeast corner of present-day Commercial and Alameda streets persists. Writers of the past, delving lightly into the archives for the Mexican period of Los Angeles history, came upon references to the Indian "ranchería of poblanos" at that spot in the old pueblo and concluded that there was the surviving Yang-na. Had these "historians" looked more deeply into the same records, they would have discovered that this *ranchería* was not Yang-na, but a segregated district with approximately a ten-year life span (1836–45) where were impounded the local Indians, most of them drifters from the secularized missions of Southern California.

The myth that Los Angeles was founded with pomp and ceremony seems indestructible. Apparently, most citizens of America's third largest city want to believe that it had a splendid beginning. The available facts, however, point to the simplest of starts—unattended by governor, officials, priests, musicians, speechmakers, or ceremonies.

When was the myth first launched? Not during the Spanish or Mexican period, so far as records show. Not in 1852, when Los Angeles presented its claim to pueblo land before the United States Board of Land Commissioners. Attorney Joseph Lancaster Brent, representing the city, offered the commissioners a copy of the regulations—the *Reglamento* —issued by Governor Felipe de Neve for the colonization of California giving detailed instructions for setting up the pueblo of Los Angeles. He offered a transcript of the proceedings by which the settlers were placed officially in possession in 1786, five years after the founding, and proof that the pueblo was raised to the rank of city in 1835. Furthermore, Brent gave evidence that, in 1850, the city was incorporated by American legislative action. While he claimed for the pueblo four-times-four square leagues, the claim was upheld to four square leagues only. Pomp and ceremony were completely absent from the account of the founding given in the first Los Angeles city directory, issued in 1872. Incidentally, this directory apparently contained the first attempt at Los Angeles city or county historiography. The ambitious history of Los Angeles published in 1876, when many American cities were observing the centennial of the Declaration of Independence in the same way, contained as simple an account of the town's beginning as did the directory—with errors, to be sure, but free of festive additions.

During the boom of the 1880's, when hordes of newcomers poured into the Los Angeles area, considerable thought was being given to historical matters. The newly started Historical Society of Southern California was flourishing. Antonio Coronel, who had come to Los Angeles in 1834, fifty-three years after the founding, and who was esteemed for his lively interest in early California customs, was being questioned by local historians eager to know about their city's beginning. In 1889, he wrote a letter to Father J. Adam concerning the founding of the city. I quote the essence of that letter: "For the solemnities of the day a temporary shelter was erected. There a solemn mass was said by the minister of Gabriel, with the aid of the choristers and musicians of said mission. There was a salvo of carbines, and a procession, with a cross, candlesticks, and the standard with the image of Our Lady of Angels, which the women carried. This procession made a circuit of the plaza, the priest blessing the plaza and the building lots distributed."

Don Antonio, then seventy-two, followed this account with a reference in his letter to the ceremony of giving possession, although the date and the name of the military officer were incorrectly stated.

If my findings are correct, Antonio Coronel is the "villain" who launched the "pomp and ceremony" myth. Where did he get it? He had not even been born when Los Angeles was founded. I suggest that his story—at complete variance with available facts—represents Los Angeles' collective memory of a different event: the fiesta of Our Lady of the Angels, celebrated, according to Bancroft, "with extra-

ordinary ceremony" on the occasion of the formal dedication of the Plaza Church. Both Los Angeles and Mission
San Gabriel joined in this affair, which took place on December 8, 1822, with José de la Guerra y Noriega chosen
by the *ayuntamiento* as "*padrino.*"

The Coronel version passed almost intact, but with improved phraseology and the addition of the governor's
presence and his speech "full of good advise," into historian
J. M. Guinn's *Historical and Biographical Record of Los
Angeles and Vicinity*, which appeared in 1901. Later in the
same year, Charles Dwight Willard incorporated the Guinn
account in his *History of Los Angeles*. Willard, a true news-
paperman, added that the ceremony "was probably the
most extensive and the most impressive that was ever held
over the founding of an American city."

Thus arose, in my opinion, a myth out of a founding as
simple as any village, any town, any city ever had anywhere.
So far as is known, eleven families and four soldiers, unac-
companied by governor, priest, choisters, or musicians, un-
packed their mules and built their first rude shelters—with
the heads of families being assigned house and farm lots.
The Willard story now dominates all later stories concerning
the founding of Los Angeles. (Consult, for proof, books on
the Los Angeles area by those two genial commentators on
the local scene, Remi Nadeau and Bill Murphy.) News-
paperman Ed Ainsworth, who loves both ceremonies and
anti-ceremonialists, says, alas, that it makes no difference
how the city was founded. Los Angeles newspapers, called
upon each year, just before September 4, to say something
nice about the founding, almost always assign the job to
fledgling reporters. These young myth-makers come up with
interesting features of their own, and when anyone is foolish
enough to collect their descriptions, an amusing potpourri

101

is the result. In the year 1962, unfortunately, the Los Angeles newspapers forgot all about the significance of September 4. Not until September 5, the day after the anniversary of the founding, did they comment on the few sorry celebrants who had gathered in Olvera Street to toast the nearly forgotten birth of their city.

The Catholic church has sometimes been accused of fostering the ceremonial myth. Actually, from Father Palou, who wrote perhaps the first account of the founding, published in 1887, to Father Maynard Geiger, California's current Franciscan historian, the church has voted for the simple story. Founding a pueblo was not a religious affair but a civil matter. It should be remembered, too, that the early Franciscan missionaries did not look favorably upon either pueblos or privately owned ranchos. Their letters continually revealed their opposition and their convictions that the Indians who worked for pueblo authorities or for *rancheros* set poor examples for mission neophytes.

The collection of material about the founding and the founders, made in 1931 by the Historical Society of Southern California, still remains the best source. It was published in one volume in commemoration of the city's one hundred and fiftieth anniversary. This collection helps to demonstrate that all facts about Los Angeles' early days are important and that the non-ceremonial simplicity of the founding of America's third largest city is in itself dramatic.

To the credit of Mayor Samuel W. Yorty, the city of Los Angeles published factual accounts of the founding in leaflet and brochure form in time for the anniversary celebration in 1965. Whether future administrations can resist the "pomp and ceremony" myth remains to be seen.

The granting of ranchos in California began in 1784. A heritage of the rancho period is the myth, believed by many

102

Angelenos as well as many other Californians, that the ranchos were created by grants received directly from the king of Spain. Whenever a descendant of a rancho-owning family dies, his obituary is apt to state that his ancestor received "a grant from the King of Spain." This pleasant notion conceives of a benevolent Spanish monarch across the seas thinking kindly of a "blue-blooded" Spanish soldier in far-away California and rewarding him with a wide valley or a vast plain upon which to graze his cattle and raise his family. Actually, the necessity of royal approval for land grants outside of pueblo or presidio boundaries in New Spain had been done away with fifteen years before Spain occupied California. Supreme authority in New Spain during the Spanish period was vested in the viceroy, who acted as the representative of the king, with his seat of office in Mexico City. Under him were military chiefs, serving as governors in the outlying territories, including California. During the Mexican regime, the governors were answerable to the central government in Mexico. In California, during both periods, the concessions or grants of ranchos came from the governors or their representatives. The one exception was the grant of Sitio de la Brea, in Santa Clara County, which came from the viceroy himself.

The myth of the capture of Joseph Chapman, the first American to come to Los Angeles, has been equally persistent. The most recent book on Los Angeles, socio-historical in treatment, preserves this story as factual. After all, it is so good it should be true. According to this story, Chapman, a member of Bouchard's coast-raiding party in 1818, was captured by being lassoed at Refugio Beach near Santa Barbara. A pretty girl, a member of the Ortega family, supposedly pleaded with his captors and saved him from being dragged to death. Naturally, he married the girl. Actually,

103

Chapman went ashore at Monterey with two companions while the city was under attack. He was arrested there and brought as a prisoner to Southern California. He became a citizen of the Los Angeles area, probably in 1821, and married an Ortega girl. The mythical aspects seem to be the creation of pioneer Angeleno Stephen C. Foster. His contribution to the Los Angeles *Express*, "First American in Los Angeles," was described by Bancroft as "an interesting sketch," but "purely fictitious so far as details are concerned." In spite of Bancroft's comment and his detailed account of the whole adventure, few historians and writers have been able to resist the happy tale.

In 1849, Los Angeles, eager to go into the real estate business, was surveyed for the first time. The survey, made by Lieutenant E. O. C. Ord, resulted in another myth that is still going strong. According to the story, Ord was offered either cash or lots in downtown Los Angeles in payment and chose cash. Quoting J. Gregg Layne, historian and delightful myth-maker: "Oh! that he [Ord] may never hear the wails of his heirs, to the third and fourth generation, for making this decision." Actually, Lieutenant Ord and the members of the City Council were equally smart. Ord, with an eye to the future, wanted cash and land. The councilmen, also looking forward to rising land values, insisted that Ord take cash only. He was paid $3,000.

Another amusing tale, a favorite of Layne's, involves the Los Angeles delegates to the first constitutional convention, held in Monterey in 1849. The delegates were Manuel Domínguez, José Antonio Carrillo, Abel Stearns, Hugo Reid, and Stephen C. Foster. According to the legend, those traveling north on horseback spent the entire time during the journey arguing over whether the world was round or flat. Domínguez was reputed to have held to the theory that the world was flat and to have asserted at every stop, "Gentlemen, I tell you she is flat!" Gregg loved to tell this yarn in the presence of members of the Domínguez family, especially if they were ladies. In fact, the story is nonsensical, for all these gentlemen represented Los Angeles at its intellectual best.

In the hide-trading days of the 1830's, a California *ranchero*'s word was as good as the best bond. The story is told of the embarrassment of Don Agustín Machado when he boarded a ship at San Pedro, coming from his nearby rancho of La Ballona, in what is now the Culver City area, to select some wanted goods. A young assistant to the shipowner, inexperienced in California customs, asked the well-to-do *ranchero* for some guaranty. Don Agustín was astonished. Realizing he was being distrusted, he pulled one hair from his beard, handed it to the young man, and said: "Here, deliver this to Señor Aguirre [the shipowner]. Tell him it is a hair from the beard of Agustín Machado."

The Joaquín Murieta myth hardly belongs to the Los Angeles area; yet the excitement over this imaginary bandit was statewide. The publication in 1854 of a small book entitled *The Life and Adventures of Joaquín Murieta*, launched California's best myth. The author was a Cherokee Indian, John R. Ridge, who wrote under the name of "Yellow Bird." Immediately, fiction became reality, and California's "Robin Hood" became the state's most popular and widely seen bandit. Murieta was said even to have visited the San Fernando Valley. He was the answer to the Californians' yearning for romance. When, a hundred years later, the University of Oklahoma Press brought out an edition, reprinted from the rare original, Joseph Henry Jackson wrote a detailed and lengthy introduction. Concluding, Jackson said that author Ridge "died at forty with

105

no inkling that the myth he had manufactured practically out of whole cloth, would be a part of his adopted state's tradition a hundred years later. . . . Since there wasn't a Murieta—at least not much of a Murieta—it was necessary to invent one."

The story of the "Feliz curse" is strictly Angeleno and the creation of Los Angeles' most eminent myth-maker, Horace Bell. Los Feliz was a Spanish rancho located within the present city limits and belonging once to members of the Feliz family. Bell accuses the highly respected Antonio Coronel of robbing the Feliz family of their rancho. A disinherited niece, Petranilla, Bell says, accordingly pronounced a fearful curse on the lands belonging to the rancho. The curse was effective and when Rancho Los Feliz finally came into the hands of Colonel Griffith J. Griffith, he hastened to rid himself of the curse-ridden acres by giving them—now Griffith Park—to the city of Los Angeles. Over the years, whenever a flood or a fire has hit Griffith Park, some young, local newspaper reporter has come excitedly upon the myth and related it as a new discovery. Actually, the "cursing" niece was well cared for by the mother of Don Antonio Feliz. In the story, Don Antonio was robbed of his rancho while on his deathbed. The larger part of the land which once belonged to the rancho—including the Silver Lake area—is now one of the older residential districts in Los Angeles and, well covered with homes, is quite immune to the curse and to the floods and fires that are normal on the chaparral-clad mountains that comprise much of Griffith Park. The myth seemed to be dying, for when a race riot occurred in the park a few years ago, not one newspaper thought to drag out the old story about the "curse." But no! A new reporter on the *Herald-Examiner* recently came across the story and gave it an extraordinary play in a Sunday issue.

Especially in the San Pascual, the Pasadena, area of the San Gabriel Valley has myth-making flowered. Myths purporting to tell the origin of "San Pascual" take many forms. In one, soldiers in the Portolá party—or even sailors far off at sea—saw the Altadena-Pasadena region blazing with poppies. Struck dumb at the sight, these pious men fell to their knees, and then arose to label the expanse "the altar cloth of Holy Easter," or San Pascual. In another form, the chief of the local Indians befriended Portolá, who was lost on his way back from the first trip north. The chief smoked a peace pipe with Portolá contrary to Gabrielino custom, and was later baptized and called "Pascual el Capitán." In still a third version of the story, the rancho was given on Easter Day, 1826, to Doña Eulalia Pérez de Guillén, famous housekeeper of the mission—despite the fact that the canny priests of San Gabriel knew they had no authority to convey titles to land. The reader can choose the story he likes best, for all versions are completely fictitious. If the reader is a realist, however, he will study the United States District Court record (now housed in the Bancroft Library, University of California at Berkeley) for a complete account of Rancho San Pascual and its ownership in the Mexican and early American periods.

The furthermost outpost of the San Gabriel Valley— Azusa—is utterly unable to free itself from myth-makers. Bill Becker, a special writer for the now non-existent *New York Times Western Edition*, wishing to do something nice for this community with the puzzling name, made his contribution through his newspaper on November 9, 1962, under the title of "Whither Azusa?" After discussing the community and dismissing one derivation of the town that "has everything from A to Z in the U.S.A.," he stated that Azusa was originally a Mexican land grant known as "El Susa Rancho." The area, he continued, was sold to an Englishman, Henry Dalton, who renamed it Azusa Rancho de Dalton.

My letter to the *New York Times* protesting the Becker-ism brought no response. In denying that there ever was a rancho named El Susa, I asked, "Why is it that no news-paperman ever consults a place-name book?" I referred to Phil Townsend Hanna's *Dictionary of California Land Names*, which had been available since 1946, and to Erwin G. Gudde's *California Place Names*, which was published in 1949. They both show Azusa to be derived from *Asuksa-gna* or *Asuka-gna*, which was a Gabrielino (Shoshonean) name for the early-day Indian village located in the area. I could have gone into much more detail, with earlier and later references to the town's Indian origins. I fear, however, that the people of Azusa must continue to bear their cross, for the general public and all newspapermen prefer foolish and mythical origins to one that is factual and logical.

The story of the great San Fernando Valley "conspiracy" should not be overlooked. According to the Morrow Mayo–Carey McWilliams school of myth-makers, a syndicate (or perhaps two syndicates) of leading Angelenos conspired with the water board of the Department of Water and Power to initiate the construction of a 250-mile-long aqueduct. This project was intended to bring water to the San Fer-nando Valley and enrich the conspirators, who held valley real estate. Usually, Harrison Gray Otis and Harry Chan-dler are named as the leading conspirators. They would be the obvious villains because of the anti-labor-union stand of their newspaper, the Los Angeles *Times*.

Actually, there were two syndicates. The San Fernando Mission Land Company, the Huntington syndicate, was headed by L. C. Brand. It bought 16,000 acres of valley land in 1904, long before the Owens Valley aqueduct plan was worked out, with the hope of profiting from Henry E. Huntington's building of an electric railway from Los Angeles to San Fernando. The other syndicate, the Los Angeles Suburban Homes Company, whose financial leader was Otto F. Brant, bought 47,500 acres of valley land from the Van Nuys group in 1909–10, hoping to benefit from the aqueduct, which was then being built, provided annexation of the San Fernando Valley to Los Angeles was possible. Counsellor Henry O'Melveny advised that annexation was feasible. Both syndicates were speculative ventures made by speculative-minded men. Both paid off—with the passage of years. The second syndicate is said to have made eight dollars for each dollar invested, a profit that would not seem overwhelmingly large in the light of later and more recent valley land transactions. My account of the "conspiracy" is based on a personal examination of the minutes taken at meetings of the board of directors for the San Fernando Mission Land Company and of the mountainous files of the Los Angeles Suburban Homes Company, on discussions with some of the principals, and on a close study of public records and newspaper stories. Historians and writers continue to stub their toes in the San Fernando Valley when dealing with questionable source material.

A personal experience illustrates well how these stories come into being. Several years ago, I turned on the television to hear and watch Frank C. Baxter on his "Harvest" program. It was devoted to California place names. One community after another was given fascinating treatment. When Baxter came to Beverly Hills, he asserted, to my dismay and with his usual relish, that the place was named for the home town of founder Burton E. Green, "Beverly Farms, Massachusetts." Now, I had made that false statement in 1938, in a brochure on Beverly Hills when I had been unable to get in touch with Mr. Green, head of the Rodeo Land and Water Company, who was busy selling real estate, and had relied on hearsay. The myth was given wide circulation through that brochure. It was picked up and included in Hanna's and Gudde's place-name books—with full personal credit. There were later editions of these basic books, and many other writers cited the fictitious origin, including Irving Stone when the magazine *Holiday* featured Beverly Hills in 1952.

Burton Green had long been disturbed over the misconception regarding the naming of his glamorous city. In a letter following the appearance of Stone's article, he wrote that he had tried to correct the story but that it continued to crop up. "Actually," he said, "the naming of Beverly Hills came about in this way: When I was trying to decide on a name for the city we were about to build, I happened to read a newspaper article which mentioned that President Taft was vacationing in Beverly Farms, Massachusetts. As I read the article, it struck me that Beverly was a pretty name. I suggested the name 'Beverly Hills' to my associates; they liked it; and the name was accepted."

When Burton Green died in May, 1965, the lengthy obituary which appeared in the Los Angeles *Times* gave an accurate account of the naming of the city. If Mr. Green could have read his own obituary, he would have had final happiness. Nevertheless, I fear that the Beverly Hills tale, which I so vigorously launched, will attain immortality. It is repeated here to illustrate how such tales originate.

All who try to tell the local story are to a degree myth-makers. It is impossible for any historian, whether of high or low degree, to get all the facts. It is impossible to maintain complete impartiality, and it is natural to yearn for romance. My hope is that I have not launched any new myths in this summary.

11

Vital City

MIKE JACKSON, *Herald-Examiner* columnist, once said, "The trouble with writing anything about Los Angeles is that by the time it sees print it is no longer quite accurate."

That statement carries the implication of a city sufficiently vital to be perpetually changing. Many citizens, and sometimes visitors, sense the city's vitality and attribute it variously to the climate, to the population pressure, to particular individuals, or to the swift flow of the freeways. "It [Los Angeles] is just beginning to pop," said Los Angeles *Times* music critic Martin Bernheimer. It has "enormous vigor," remarked Philadelphia's planning director, Edmund Bacon. He added that the city is "being shaped on a vast new scale, and you have the freeways to thank for it." A fairly recent arrival from New York, Maurice Tuchman, curator of modern art at the Los Angeles County Museum of Art, put on, in the summer of 1967, a sensational show which may be a landmark in "American Sculpture of the Sixties." Tuchman is pushing a project that envisions the marriage of industrial technology and art through an effort "to revamp the face of America, starting with California." Such plans frequently overwhelm Angelenos, both newly

112

arrived and old-time residents. They tend to become fever-ish—frenzied in thought and action.

Novelist Robert Carson, long a participant in Holly-wood's activities, says, "The place is jumping . . . . It has a vitality and pace and unrelenting pressure only Manhattan can match." Architect William Pereira is of the opinion that "more and more architects are getting more oppor-tunities to do exciting things here than anywhere else." For sport fans, Los Angeles is perhaps *the* sports center. For musicians, it is a most pleasurable and expanding world, with musical events drawing almost as well as baseball. "What we have here," said Sean O'Faolain, "is a wonder-ful vessel, a genuinely new shape of urban life, waiting to be filled."

Coming down to earth after these emotional outbursts, it does seem accurate to say that Los Angeles has been a vital city for many years. Its vitality has expressed itself sometimes boldly and significantly, sometimes extrava-gantly and foolishly, sometimes in boosting, sometimes in boasting.

Striking examples of the city's vitality and ingenuity in-clude the creation and construction of aqueducts which bring water from great distances to Los Angeles, of a deep-water harbor at San Pedro which has become the most important port for the Southwest, and of an intricate and embracing freeway system which has given Los Angeles the sinews of a supercity. Right now, the city's all-out fight against smog is serving as a national guide in combating air pollution. The series of redevelopment projects under way, while not unique, indicate the vital steps being taken by local citizens towards transformation of older sections of the Los Angeles area. Likewise, Angelenos and Southern Cali-fornians are drawing increasingly upon "regional land use

113

consultants" and "environmental architects" when planning newer communities. Designers have provided for schools, shopping centers, churches, recreation clubs, parks, promenades, and even light industries.

A different type of exuberance characterized Los Angeles during past real estate booms, especially those of the 1880's and the 1920's. The words "extravagant," "foolish," "boost," and "boast" have special relevance in describing the periods from 1887–88 and 1920–24.

During the eighties, the railroads, with Southern California land to sell, persuaded thousands of persons in the eastern United States to move west. In the Los Angeles area, the selling of lots and acreage took place at the curb, in saloons, in restaurants, on the tract, and at all hours of the day and night, with people standing in line to buy. New towns featuring new hotels and colleges sprang up along the railways. Elephants, human freaks, free lunches, bands, and excursions were used to draw crowds. A flood of buyers, subdividers, builders, and salesmen moved into Southern California. Silver-tongued, silk-hatted orators conducted real estate auctions at the openings of subdivisions and towns.

"Salt one down for your baby or your young wife," was the advice given on the E-L-A Tract in Los Angeles. "Here the flowers bloom with brighter tint and sweeter perfume, the fruits have a richer hue and finer flavor" was Altadena's claim. Dundee, in the San Fernando Valley, had, it was asserted, "the grandest scenery, the most productive soil, the healthiest climate." Promoters of the Yorba & Paige Tract, located on the "main thoroughfare to Pasadena and Alhambra," proclaimed that "a cool and gentle breeze wafts over it everlastingly during summer." A salesman-prophet wrote, "No new town in Southern California has

114

brighter prospects for becoming a railroad center than South Cucamonga."

Because of this particular boom, the United States never forgot that good climate, good soil, and water for development were available in the southwestern corner of the country. Nor did Southern California ever outgrow its reputation as a booster, a boaster, a user of extravagant language. The colorful, dramatic, mustachioed Frank Wiggins, who went west to die but lived to become secretary and manager of the Los Angeles Chamber of Commerce, helped make Los Angeles famous through that organization, which played a vital role in developing Southern California. The Chamber of Commerce was once all it was thought to be. Today it is a sober, fact-gathering organization. The more colorful boosting activities have been appropriated by the All-Year-Club—and that club's financial wings have been clipped recently.

For a few years following 1920, every state in the Union contributed to the western migration, by automobile, that each year brought one hundred thousand people into Los Angeles alone. Advertising was as fantastic during the boom of the 1920's as it had been in the 1880's, but two features were added, both results of the dominance of the automobile. One new feature was the development and promotion of beach clubs, golf clubs, trout clubs, salt-water swimming clubs, and various artists' clubs—all with club-houses to be reached by automobile. The other was the free bus ride to a distant real estate tract to hear a broker's spiel. It was not difficult to arrange such a trip; in fact, it was hard not to, for solicitors stood at strategic downtown spots with tickets in their extended hands. The climax to such a ride was reached at the tract, when with megaphone in hand, the salesman proclaimed—and this is a direct quotation:

115

"My only wish is that you could appreciate with the same certainty that I do the good fortune in store for you. Follow my advice and buy one, or ten of these lots, regardless of the sacrifice it might mean. Ten thousand banks may close, stocks may smash, bonds may shrink to little or nothing, but this tract and Los Angeles real estate stand like the Rock of Gibraltar for safety, certainty and profit. Don't be satisfied with six per cent on your money. Don't be satisfied with twelve per cent. Buy property like this and keep it, and as sure as the world moves it will pay you one hundred per cent to one thousand per cent and more per annum. Be among those who earn from one hundred per cent to ten thousand per cent. We offer you this opportunity."

The thousands of newcomers who streamed into the Los Angeles area in the 1920's and 1930's, mostly people up-rooted from their normal activities, expressed a different type of vitality in their furious eagerness for unconventional religious nostrums, for utopian political schemes, and for grandiose, speculative ventures. Books have been written about these effusions of vitality, with a variety of reasons for their prevalence in Los Angeles. Today they have more historical than current significance.

In the area of unconventional religious interests, there were the theosophical followers of Katherine Tingley; the colonists of Krotona; the New Thoughters; the devotees of faith-healers, notably of Aimee Semple McPherson; the cultists who subscribed to the doctrines of the Mighty I Am and of Mankind United; and the numerous organizations dedicated to matters psychic, occult, or pertaining to Indian mysticism.

In Los Angeles there was a huge flourishing of crack pot utopian politics. The mysterious and temporary Decimo Club in the late 1920's, with a membership fee of $10.00

116

and an implied threat to non-joiners, offered a vague co-operative plan for Decimos to get or keep jobs and to buy commodities cheap. The depression in the 1930's, however, really set off an explosion of such movements. There were the Technocrats, promoted locally by the *Daily News* publisher, Manchester Boddy. Later came the Utopian Society, started by three Californians to "provide and guarantee economic security to every man, woman and child in America." This was a sort of secret, fraternal group which held neighborhood meetings throughout Los Angeles and built up a membership of half a million persons. Upton Sinclair, in his EPIC (End Poverty in California) movement, nearly captured the governorship of the state. Launched in Long Beach by Dr. Francis Townsend was the Townsend Pension Plan, which promised $200.00 a month to oldsters—provided they spent this sum monthly. The "Ham and Eggs for Californians" movement offered $30.00 a week for life to persons over fifty years of age. This originated in a plan of "$25.00 every Monday," set in motion by Robert Noble, one-time follower of Huey Long and taken over by the Allen brothers, Willis and Lawrence, who changed the slogan to "$30.00 every Thursday." All that remains of these expressions of misdirected energy are the incredible examples of promotional literature—booklets, leaflets, and newspapers—that today are sought by collectors.

Los Angeles was the scene of a series of financial fiascos, largely related to the frantic speculations in oil and real estate that followed the mass migration of people to Southern California in the early 1920's or that stemmed from the depression of the 1930's. The receivership of the Richfield Oil Company of California; the failure of the Guaranty Building & Loan Association, the American Mortgage Company of California, and the Harold G. Ferguson Cor-

117

poration; and the liquidation of The Pacific Mutual Life Insurance Company of California are easily recollected by Angelenos.

Most spectacular of the disastrous financial schemes was the earlier affair involving the Julian Petroleum Corporation. The receivership and reorganization of this corporation was the prelude to a series of corporate receiverships, liquidations, and rehabilitations. C. C. Julian was a Texas oil rigger who migrated to Los Angeles without a dime. In 1922, he obtained a ten-acre oil lease near the discovery well at Santa Fe Springs and invited the public to join him and get rich. The public, liking his sensational and folksy advertising copy, clamored to become stockholders in Julian's company. Julian expanded, and the expansion called for more and more money. When local bankers turned down his requests for loans, they became "crooks," "con men," and "pawnbrokers." Meanwhile his own adventures in extravagance—he bought a gold-lined bathtub and tipped a cabbie $1,500—made headlines. When Julian Petroleum Corporation got into financial trouble, newcomers, who were better at borrowing than C. C., took over and organized stock pools and a stock flotation—ultimately involving forged stock certificates—that drew forty thousand victims into a giant swirl of fraud. Men high in social and financial circles became members of the pools, and the aftermath was sensational. Indictments were issued against key figures. The district attorney was found guilty of accepting bribes, and he and the chief promoters went to prison. A prominent banker was shot and killed in a Los Angeles courtroom. Other bankers found it necessary to "retire" from their official positions. In the reorganization of the Julian corporation, stockholders received partial satisfaction for their claims. C. C. Julian, penniless, committed suicide in Shanghai.

Current enthusiasm among Angelenos for exhibitionist religions, utopian politics, and wild speculation is not markedly different from that found among citizens of other large cities. Perhaps Los Angeles has "had it." It is no longer the pitchman's paradise. The "nut" aspects are largely of the past, although it is still possible for a visitor in downtown Los Angeles to see a stentorian-voiced walker holding a Bible aloft and shouting so loud he can be heard for three blocks: "Read the Bible! Read the Bible!"

People of the Los Angeles area now find a partial outlet for their vitality in surfing, baseball, horse racing, skiing, football, golf, yachting, motorcycling, and other sports. In the naturally water-poor region are countless privately owned swimming pools well used by restless Angelenos, who live fifty-five minutes from a destination rather than fifty-five miles. The average middle-aged Angeleno is possibly a somewhat rootless individual with a vague yearning for culture. He believes in the eternal, dizzying present and is a three-car family man who loves "cookouts" and sport clothes.

The average Angeleno patronizes several of the thousands of restaurants that flourish in the area and thinks nothing of driving thirty to forty miles to his favorite place. These distances defeat attempts by national magazine writers to make restaurant awards. The usual practice among such writers is to repeat in rewritten form the items on the list from the preceding year or to visit places in close proximity to their hotel headquarters. In 1967, *Holiday* magazine gave "special awards" to Perino's, Restaurant La Rue, Scandia, Chasen's, The Windsor, Au Petit Jean, and

119

La Bella Fontana—with the "recommended" additions of The Tower, La Scala, The Bistro, Don the Beachcomber, The Cove, Eve's, King's Four-in-Hand, L'Auberge, New Hung Far, and André's, all places of easy access. A young Hollywood star or starlet patronizes a private club like The Daisy in Beverly Hills. For a teenager, the rendezvous will most likely be a spot on the Sunset Boulevard Strip. Essentially, the Los Angeles area is still a place of single-family homes, rather than of apartment houses and hotels. Therefore, it is not a "restaurant town" in the sense of San Francisco or New York, although admittedly it has good restaurants patronized heavily by a Hollywood clientele.

The Los Angeles approach to burial has influenced the entire country. Forest Lawn, notably satirized by Evelyn Waugh in *The Loved One*, has profoundly affected the habits of the morticians of the nation and their "clients." Founder Hubert Eaton revolutionized cemetery development when he coined the term "memorial park" and introduced the mortuary-within-a-cemetery concept. He improved burial practices; adopted the use of lawn-level bronze plates as grave markers instead of granite tombstones; built churches within the cemetery confines; displayed sculptured figures, mosaics, stained glass, and paintings; and launched the "pre-need" plan for buying burial space and for making advance arrangements. Today morticians from outside Los Angeles make pilgrimages to Forest Lawn to study the fine points of methodology, and there is widespread imitation among funeral directors in and outside of Los Angeles. Annually more than one million visitors interested in Southern California's most distinguished necropolis visit Forest Lawn. The average Angeleno likes the looks of the green slopes, accepts the imported

120

art, admires the suavity with which funerals are handled, and hopes he can afford to be buried there.

Master planning is an important current activity in the Los Angeles area. Reference has already been made to consultants, engineers, and architects who plan cities within cities or design complete communities to be built on the land that once belonged to the old Spanish and Mexican ranchos. Outstanding examples include "Century City," a high-rise entity within Los Angeles; "Valencia," taking shape on nearby Rancho San Francisco; and the "Irvine Ranch" development in Orange County, a vast undertaking encompassing seashore living, a major university campus (University of California at Irvine), numbers of agreeable residential areas and industrial regions—these are many-faceted complexes master-planned by nationally known architectural and engineering firms.

Another phase of master planning, one of over-all signif-icance, is that being undertaken by the Los Angeles City Planning Department. The co-operation of affected city agencies and of the public itself is being sought in the department's attempts to identify and determine goals. Existing plans are being compiled into a single document and updated. The final result of the department's efforts, it is hoped, will be a comprehensive master plan for Los Angeles, designed—through constant updating and revision—to guide Los Angeles' physical growth in the decades ahead. This master plan, assembled in an approved package, will apply to the entire metropolitan region and will involve land use and open-space objectives, population distribution, and traffic movements, together with zoning and subdivision control.

In 1781, Los Angeles was a carefully planned Spanish

pueblo, but as it grew, it outgrew original and later plans. The first mapping and subdivision of the heart of the pueblo took place in 1849. For many decades afterward, Angelenos, uncontrolled by prescribed patterns of subdividing and selling, built what they wanted, where they wanted, and for any purpose. A beginning attempt at zoning was made in 1904, when the city was divided into residential and industrial districts. There was increased, though always belated, control over subdivision and sales procedures. In 1920 the first planning commission was established, and in 1941 a zoning administration was created. Official recognition of planning as a developing science became apparent by the middle of the 1950's. In 1965, Calvin S. Hamilton was brought from Pittsburgh to fill the office of city planning director.

Los Angeles, the happy home of the bulldozer, has attained fame through "man's prodigal meddling with his environment," to quote author Richard G. Lillard's devastating phrase. Master planning is really an attempt to restore order to the chaos stemming from population explosion. Whether the job has been undertaken too late remains to be seen.

"Los Angeles Beautiful," is a citizens' organization that since 1949 has helped stem the tide of urban ugliness. It has planted hundreds of thousands of trees, with a most agreeable effect on downtown Los Angeles, has helped keep freeways clear of billboards and vacant lots free of rubbish; has launched an anti-litter campaign, and has landscaped the grounds of industrial plants, businesses, and public buildings. The coral tree (Erythrina) was dedicated by Mayor Samuel W. Yorty as the city's official tree.

Three hundred and forty communities look to the "Los Angeles Beautiful" group for advice. The present program includes planning for the bicentennial year of 1969, the two-hundredth anniversary of Spanish occupation of California, when it is hoped that the southern part of the state, through its plantings, will be blanketed with a blaze of color. The guiding spirit of "Los Angeles Beautiful" is and has been a dedicated woman, Valley M. Knudsen, president, who freely admits Los Angeles is ugly but believes it is improving.

From the large-scale aircraft industry which got its start in the area during World War II, have grown the space research and missiles industries. Research scientists, engineers, and technicians have been drawn to Southern California and have helped make it the electronics and space-age center of the United States. Huge industrial plants in the San Fernando Valley, missile test centers located in out-of-the-way spots, centers of research, "think factories" like Santa Monica's RAND Corporation and Pasadena's Jet Propulsion Laboratory at the California Institute of Technology—these industries are the products of a specialized type of migration. The aerospace industry is a lively and significant Southern California activity, showing, as pointed out by the *New Yorker* commentator, Christopher Rand, "an inventiveness and a technological artistry not unlike the old Hollywood's." Between ten and twelve thousand local firms are said to serve this industry, which has unlimited possibilities in the vital city of Los Angeles.

Perhaps no city in the United States has inspired, over the years, as much pungent comment from visitors as has Los Angeles. Yet, today this "front-page" megalopolis, which has drawn to its confines some of the best talents of the world and whose far-flung freeways are its sinews, has

123

developed into one of the nation's most mobile and advanced urban areas.

Los Angeles, spread-eagling in all directions, today serves as a living laboratory for urban observers everywhere. Admittedly, it has meddled with its environment. It has polluted the air, the sea, and the scenery, and has even bulldozed away most of its orange groves. Nevertheless, Los Angeles' continuing activities in facing or solving fundamental and contemporary city problems help make this motorized area one of the centers of civilization. And the massive impact of Hollywood on the manners, morals, and thinking of the United States and the world continues to assure this status.

In this small volume, I have attempted to set forth the "why" of the wholesale migrations of people to Southern California. I have even tried to answer the basic question of why there is a Los Angeles. But I have not intended this book to be a history, even though I tell of the city's Spanish-Mexican heritage and of past explosions of racial tensions. Instead, I have tried to make this book an interpretation of a modern city, based on a description of the forces which have molded it and which have created the problems which today Los Angeles is attempting to solve. And as cities grow ever larger, a greater number of people look to Los Angeles for imaginative solutions.

Books About Los Angeles

RATHER THAN LISTING one hundred books and calling the list "The Los Angeles Hundred," I am mentioning only a few publications, with comments on each of them. I hope this method will serve the present purpose better than a conventional or even a "selective" bibliography.

No adequate, adult history of Los Angeles exists in book form today. Perhaps Los Angeles is not yet at the stage where a full history is wanted by publishers or the public. Of course, the histories of the state of California from Hubert Howe Bancroft to John Walton Caughey and Andrew F. Rolle contain vital Los Angeles historical material. Other purported histories of Los Angeles are either juvenile or completely out of date.

What is easily available, however, in the nonfiction field, is a lengthy list of books, each covering aspects of Los Angeles, including the habits and morals of Angelenos. Los Angeles has served as the background setting for many novels, but it has inspired little good fiction. No attempt has been made here to discuss short stories in which the Los Angeles plays a part.

In referring to the nonfiction books, I think at once of

Robert Glass Cleland's *The Cattle on a Thousand Hills* (1941), devoted to Southern California's pastoral period, and of Glenn S. Dumke's *The Boom of the Eighties in Southern California* (1944). Both books were published by the Huntington Library and were written in an informal style, although the results of scholarly research. Both have been reprinted. *Music in the Southwest* (1952), by Howard Swann, is another Huntington Library publication, covering both the theater and music. It is a useful and interesting volume.

Four recent books dealing with other Los Angeles phases are important. Richard G. Lillard's *Eden in Jeopardy* (1966), an Alfred A. Knopf publication, gives a revealing portrayal of what man, without master planning, can do and has done to his environment. Los Angeles is Lillard's home town, and the author is experienced in battling fire and flood and a continuing inundation of people into his city. Another dose of strong medicine can be found in Edwin Pitt's *The Decline of the Californios* (1966). In this University of California Press publication, Pitt tells of what happened to the Spanish-speaking Californians—with emphasis on Southern Californians—following their confrontation, beginning in 1846, with immigrant Anglos. In a more optimistic mood is John L. Chapman's *Incredible Los Angeles* (1967), published by Harper & Row. This book is a lively attempt to gain perspective in looking at Los Angeles. Chapman has been an Angeleno since 1961. Christopher Rand's *Los Angeles, the Ultimate City* (1967), published by Oxford University Press, is an interpretation by a "foreigner"—that is, a New Yorker—and is particularly good in its dealing with the aerospace industry.

Remi Nadeau's *The Water Seekers* (1950), published by Doubleday, is the first authentic account of Los Angeles' search for water, the city's life blood. In this vividly written book, the author relies on original sources. Another aspect of the Los Angeles scene is covered in my book, *Lawyers of Los Angeles* (1959) published by the Los Angeles Bar Association, a history of the bar. Franklin Walker's *A Literary History of Southern California* (1950), published by the University of California Press, is useful. A lavish and revealing presentation of the art collections in Los Angeles can be found in the Lane Magazine & Book Company's *Art Treasures in the West* (1966).

An older book, Beatrice Griffith's *American Me* (1948), published by Houghton Mifflin, is a revealing and sympathetic presentation of Los Angeles' Mexican-Americans, who make up a large portion of the city's population. *Violence in the City: An End or a Beginning?* is a carefully prepared, significant report by the Governor's Commission on the Los Angeles Riots, the so-called Watts Riots, of August, 1965. The commission's chairman was John A. McCone. There are several other books or brochures on these riots—the "Los Angeles Rebellion," as some of the more radical Negroes like to designate the dreadful affair. But the commission's report is the most important, although not the most extensively illustrated. Richard M. Elman's *Ill-At-Ease in Compton* (1967), published by Pantheon Books, is a meaningful description of attitudes in a rather undistinguished town in the Los Angeles area that has recently become 60 per cent Negro and 25 per cent people of Mexican ancestry.

Hollywood has received the most noticeable treatment by writers and publishers. Chapter Five, "Hollywood Impact," discusses this subject. It is my opinion that Budd Schulberg's *What Makes Sammy Run* (1941) is the best Hollywood novel; that Arthur Knight's *The Liveliest Art* (1957) is the best non-fictional, non-technical book on Hollywood; that Hortense Powdermaker's *Hollywood, the Dream Factory* (1951) is the most sophisticated analysis of Hollywooodites; and that Gene Fowler's *Minutes of the Last Meeting* (1954) is the most entertaining of the Hollywood products.

Still other topics concerning Los Angeles are covered: the story of the development of government in *Southern California Metropolis* (1963), written by Winston W. Crouch and Beatrice Dinerman and published by the University of California Press; the accounts of several killings in *Los Angeles Murders*, written by a group of authors, each of whom specialized on a particular gruesome killing (1947), published by Duell, Sloan & Pearce, and the story of prostitution in the book *Call House Madam* (1942).

Some of the most useful books for Angelenos are not limited in scope to the Los Angeles area. Examples are Erwin G. Gudde's *California Place Names* (1949), published by the University of California Press, and Phil Townsend Hanna's *The Dictionary of California Land Names* (1946), published by the Automobile Club of Southern California. These are self-explanatory volumes and both have been updated. The delightfully presented *Conspicuous California Plants* (1938), written by Ralph D. Cornell and published by the San Pasqual Press, and *The Elfin Forest* (1923), written by Francis M. Fultz and published by the Times-Mirror Press, the latter devoted to the chaparral country, cover the botanical world. Both books treat Los Angeles areas, and both are hard to find. The Southern California mountains and deserts are discussed in Russ Leadabrand's paperback guidebooks, published by The Ward Ritchie Press. These books blend history and valuable current comment.

128

John E. Baur's *The Health Seekers of Southern California, 1870–1900* (1959), published by the Huntington Library is an important addition to the Los Angeles story.

A frank and interesting appraisal of the Los Angeles architectural scene is contained in *A Guide to Architecture in Southern California* (1965), put out by the Los Angeles County Museum of Art and written by David Gebhard and Robert Winter.

Basic to the story of Los Angeles is Bernice Eastman Johnston's *California's Gabrielino Indians* (1962), published by the Southwest Museum. This book is devoted to the brown-skinned people who preceded the Spanish, Mexicans, and Anglos to the Los Angeles area.

Part of the history of rancho days is preserved in Robert Cameron Gillingham's *The Rancho San Pedro* (1967), which details the story of one Spanish rancho—California's first. In a lighter vein are two fascinating volumes about the ranchos: Susanna Bryant Dakin's *A Scotch Paisano* (1939), published by the University of California Press— the story of Hugo Reid, who appeared on the Los Angeles scene in 1832 and who contributed to its development— and Sarah Bixby Smith's *Adobe Days* (1931), published by Jake Zeitlin, which includes a personal account of life on the ranchos Los Cerritos and Los Alamitos and of early-day impressions of Los Angeles.

Lawrence Clark Powell, one of the nation's best essayists, gives felicitous treatment to the Los Angeles area in his *Books West Southwest* (1957), published by The Ward Ritchie Press, in his *The Little Package* (1964), published by the World Publishing Company, and in his foreword to *The Raymond Chandler Omnibus* (1964), published by Alfred Knopf.

Besides the many books covering the more limited aspects of Los Angeles, there are many distinguished books of a more general nature.

One of these books, an invaluable source for the local historian, is Harris Newmark's *Sixty Years in Southern California* (1916), published by Houghton Mifflin, a year-by-year account of Los Angeles from 1853 to 1913. It is a little known fact that, from a thin, unpretentious brochure written by Harris Newmark—at first projected by the Newmark family as a private publication—this material was developed by Dr. Perry Worden into a 754-page volume. For this work, ghost-writer Worden spent three years in original research, largely going through the files of newspapers with the sponsorship and approval of Harris Newmark and his sons Maurice and Marco Newmark. For localists such as myself, the volume has an engaging style. The author gives the impression that he is actually recording important Los Angeles events as they occurred. However, the book has less appeal or significance to the non-historian.

For pleasurable reading, many Angelenos think that Horace Bell's exuberant *Reminiscences of a Ranger* (1881) is perhaps the best book about Los Angeles. It concerns itself mostly with the 1850's, when the town was bawdy, brawling, and lawless and when Bell himself was a handsome young fellow who rode the streets on a black stallion with all the silver and leather trappings of a *Californio*. It is flamboyant in style, loaded with tall tales, and full of the gusto of frontier life.

Probably Carey McWilliams has made the most thorough analysis of the whys and wherefores of Los Angeles and Southern California. His *Southern California Country* (1946), published by Duell, Sloan & Pearce, is described by Lawrence Clark Powell as "incomparably the area's best work of non-fiction." The book is well written, imaginative, dramatic, critical, and entertaining. The author, however, is a crusader rather than an objective historian, and his reliance on sensational or partisan sources occasionally leads him into false appraisals and erroneous conclusions. Otherwise, I would join Dr. Powell in acclaim. The most recent book on the city is *Los Angeles–Portrait of an Extraordinary City* (1968), the Lane Magazine and Book Company's pictorial presentation in a lavish and important volume compiled by the editors of *Sunset Books* and *Sunset Magazine*.

Two bibliographies of books on Los Angeles and Southern California have been mentioned in the text: *Books of the Los Angeles District* (1950), a non-fictional coverage, was written by J. Gregg Layne and published by Dawson's Book Shop, and *Land of Fiction* (1952) was written by Lawrence Clark Powell and also published by Dawson's. In the former book, the entries are of interest largely to collectors and specialists. The entries generally include pieces on the city's history or background and rare items. Those entries having broader scope I have mentioned here. In the latter book, high ratings are given by Powell to four novels: Helen Hunt Jackson's famous and perennial *Ramona* (1884), Budd Schulberg's Hollywood work, F. Scott Fitzgerald's *The Last Tycoon* (1941), and Raymond Chandler's *Farewell, My Lovely* (1940), a mystery story which brings Los Angeles "into focus."

Unfortunately, many of the good non-fictional books about Los Angeles need updating. Los Angeles commentaries are out of date almost as soon as written. Hence, there is a continual need for more books on Los Angeles—fictional as well as non-fictional—to keep the city in perspective and to make Angelenos aware of their complex problems.

Index

Adam, Father J.: 100
Adobe de Palomares: 78–79
Aguirre (shipowner): 105
Ahmanson Theatre: 59
Ainsworth, Ed: 101
Alger, Horatio: 16, 42
Allen, Lawrence: 117
Allen, Willis: 117
Alvarado, María Ygnacia: 56
American Me: 49
Astor, Mary: 40
Avila family: 75
Avila House: 75–76
Azusa: 107–108

Bacon, Edmund: 112
Baldwin, Lucky: 77
Bancroft, Hubert Howe: 100, 104
Barnsdall, Aline: 66
Bassett, James: 88
Baxter, Frank C.: 109
Becker, Bill: 107–108
Becket, Welton: 59
Beebe, Lucius: 4
Behymer, L. E.: 58
Belasco Theater: 58
Bell, Horace: 46, 106
Bennett, Paul A.: 66
Bernheimer, Martin: 112
Beverly Farms, Massachusetts: 110
Beverly Hills: 109–10

Bixby, Fred H.: 81
Bixby family: 80f.
*Bookman's View of Los Angeles,
A*: 66
Books of the Los Angeles District:
68
Bordwell, Judge: 93f.
Bradbury Building: 64
Brand, L. C.: 109
Brant, Otto E.: 109
Brent, Joseph Lancaster: 99
Bullock's (department store): 31
Brown, Dave: 47
Brown, Gilmor: 58
Brown, Governor Pat: 51
Bunker Hill: 24
Burbank Theater: 58
Burns, George: 40
Burns, William J.: 92

Cabrillo, Juan: 98
Caen, Herb: 4–5
Cajon Pass: 10–11
California Place Names: 108
Carr, Harry: 91
Carrillo, José Antonio: 104
Carrillo family: 75
Carson, Robert: 40, 113
Carter, Artie Mason: 58
Casa de Adobe: 82–83
Casa de Rancho Los Cerritos: 79ff.

133

Casey, Albert V.: 89
Celis, Eulogio de: 81
Central City: 6, 19, 27–28, 33
Champlin, Charles: 35, 37, 38, 97
Chandler, Dorothy Buffman: 59, 88
Chandler, Harry: 88, 95, 108
Chandler, Norman: 88, 89, 95
Chandler, Otis: 85, 87ff., 95
Chaplin, Charlie: 40
Chaplin, Lita Grey: 41
Chapman, Joseph: 103–104
Charlie Chaplin: 40
Chinatown: 47
Chisholm, Joe: 15
Civic Center: 23–24, 58
Civic Center Orchestra: 63
Civic Light Opera: 59
Clark, William A., Jr.: 58
Clarke, E. P.: 91
Cleland, Robert G.: 91
Coates, Paul: 5
Cohn, Alfred: 15
Cohn, Harry: 42
Columbia Pictures: 42
Community Playhouse (Pasadena): 58f.
Conrad, Paul: 86
Coronel, Antonio: 100, 101, 106
Crowther, Bosley: 41

Daily News: 117
Dalton, Henry: 108
Darrow, Clarence: 93f.
Dasmann, Raymond: 9
David, Leon Thomas: 48
Davis, Bette: 40
Day of the Locust, The: 43
Delaplane, Stan: 5
Del Valle family: 75
De Mille, Cecil B.: 41
De Mille, William C.: 41
Destruction of California: 9
Díaz, José: 49–50
Dictionary of California Land Names: 108
Dietrich, Marlene: 39
Disneyland: 82
Domínguez, Manuel: 104f.

Dorothy Chandler Pavilion: 58–59
Dryden, John: 69
Dudley, George: 5

Eagle Rock: 64
Eaton, Hubert: 120
Eden in Jeopardy: 5
Elman, Richard: 5
Encino Oak: 64
Evans, Dale: 40

Fairbanks, Douglas, Jr.: 40
Fairbanks, Douglas, Sr.: 40
Falkenstein, Claire: 60
Feliz, Don Antonio: 106
Fitzgerald, F. Scott: 43
Flynn, Errol: 41
Forest Lawn: 120–21
Fortune: 5
Foster, Stephen C.: 104
Fowler, Gene: 41
Fredericks (district attorney): 94
Frye (senator from Maine): 15–16

Gabor, Eva: 40–41
Garbo, Greta: 41
Gebhard, David: 64
Geiger, Father Maynard: 102
Gill, Eric: 69
Gill, Irving: 65
Gillespie, Captain: 45
Gish, Lillian: 41
Glynn, Elinor: 41
Goldwater, Barry: 86
Gompers, Samuel: 93
Good Fellows Grotto: 32–33
Good Night, Sweet Prince: 41
Grand Opera House: 57
Greek Theatre: 60
Green, Burton E.: 110
Greene, Charles Sumner: 65
Greene, Henry Mather: 65
Griffith, Beatrice: 48–49
Griffith, D. W.: 37
Griffith, Colonel Griffith J.: 106
Gudde, Erwin G.: 108
Guide to Architecture in Southern California, A: 64

Guillén, Doña Eulalia Pérez de: 107
Guinn, J. M.: 101

Hamilton, Calvin S.: 122
Hampton, Benjamin B.: 40
Hanna, Phil Townsend: 108
Hardison, Wallace: 90
Harlow, Jean: 41
Harriman, Joe: 94
Hazard's Pavilion: 57f.
Heart of Maryland, The: 90
Hebert, Ray: 97
Henry, Bill: 23, 97
Henry E. Huntington Library and Art Gallery: 69
Historical and Biographical Record of Los Angeles and Vicinity: 101
History of Los Angeles: 101
History of the Movies, A: 40
Hoja Volante: 67
Holiday: 23, 110, 119
Hollyhock House: 64, 65
Hollywood: 8, 35–43
Hollywood, the Dream Factory: 42
Hollywood: The Movie Colony, The Movie Makers: 41
Hollywood Bowl: 55, 58f., 82
Hollywood Rajah: 42
Hopper, Hedda: 41f.
Horsley, David: 36–37
Huff, Theodore: 40
Hugo Reid Adobe: 77
Huntington, Collis P.: 15–16
Huntington, Henry E.: 27, 109
Huntington Hartford Theatre: 60
Huxley, Aldous: 68

Ill-At-Ease in Compton: 5

Jackson, Joseph Henry: 105–106
Jackson, Mike: 112
Julian, C. C.: 118–19
Junior Arts Center and Gallery: 63

King Cohn: 42
Kirsch, Robert: 87, 97
Knight, Arthur: 40

Knudsen, Valley M.: 123
Kuh, Katharine: 60f.

Laemmle, Carl: 41
La Guerra y Noriega, José de: 101
Lambert, Gavin: 41
Land of Fiction: 68
La Osa, Don Vicente de: 81
Last Tycoon, The: 43
Law and Lawyers: 48
Layne, J. Gregg: 68, 104f.
Leonis Adobe: 64, 81
Life: 60
Life and Adventures of Joaquín Murieta, The: 105
Lillard, Richard G.: 5, 122
Lion's Share, The: 41
Lippman, Walter: 50
Liveliest Art, The: 40
Llewellyn Iron Works, bombing of: 93
Lloyd, Harold: 41
Long, Huey: 117
Los Angeles: versus San Francisco, 4–5; as model for the future, 5, 7–8; freeway system of, 6, 18–19, 23, 34; history of, 9–17; water sources of, 12–14; trade at, 17; smog problem of, 19–23; decentralization of, 28–29; real estate booms in, 29–32, 114–16; planned communities in, 33; racial problems of, 44–54; music in, 56–60; drama in, 57–60; art in, 60–63; architecture of, 64–66; books and printing in, 66–67; writers in, 68; libraries in, 69–70; colleges and universities in, 70; historical societies of, 70–72; pueblo of, 73–76; ranchos of, 73–83, 102–103; restaurants in, 119–20; city planning in, 121–23; science and technology in, 123; as problem solver, 124
Los Angeles County Museum of Art: 58, 60–61, 64, 82, 112
Los Angeles County Museum of Natural History: 70

Los Angeles *Examiner*: 87
Los Angeles *Express*: 104
Los Angeles *Herald*: 90
Los Angeles *Herald-Examiner*: 87, 95, 106–107, 112
Los Angeles Philharmonic Orchestra: 55, 58f.
Los Angeles Public Library: 69
Los Angeles *Star*: 81
Los Angeles State and County Arboretum: 76–77
Los Angeles Theater: 58, 90
Los Angeles *Times*: 4, 15f., 23, 35, 38, 108, 110, 112; history of, 85–97; fights labor unions, 91–94
Loved One, The: 120
Lugo, Don Antonio María: 81–82, 83
Lugo Case: 46–47
Lugo family: 75, 83
Lytton, Bart: 61
Lytton Center of the Visual Arts: 61

McCone, John A.: 51
Macdonald-Wright, Stanton: 62
Machado, Don Agustín: 105
McKinley, President William: 16
McLaglen, Victor: 41
McManigal, Ortie: 92f.
McNamara, James B.: 92–94
McNamara, John J.: 92–94
McPherson, Aimee Semple: 116
McWilliams, Carey: 50, 108
Magic Lantern, The: 40
Mann, Thomas: 68
Marineland: 82
Mark Taper Forum: 59
Marks, Lillian: 66
Marks, Saul: 66
Marx, "Groucho": 41
Mason Opera House: 58
Mayo, Morrow: 108
Mehta, Zubin: 59
Merced Theater: 57
Merrild, Knud: 62
Merton of the Movies: 42
Metro-Goldwyn-Mayer: 35, 41

Meyer, Larry: 6
Million and One Nights, A: 40
Minutes of the Last Meeting: 41
Morosco, Oliver: 58
Motion pictures: 36–40, 55
Movies in the Age of Innocence, The: 41
Mulholland, William: 13
Municipal Art Gallery: 63
Murieta, Joaquín: 105–106
Murphy, Bill: 101
Murphy, Franklin D.: 89
Murray, Jim: 97
Music Center for the Performing Arts: 58ff.
Music in the Southwest: 57
My Autobiography: 40
My Wicked, Wicked Ways: 41

Nadeau, Remi: 101
Nestor Film Company: 36–37
Neutra, Richard I.: 66
Neve, Governor Felipe de: 99
New American Press: 89
New York Times: 88, 89, 108
New York Times Book Review: 64
New York Times Western Edition: 107–108
New Yorker: 5, 123
Nixon, Richard: 86
Noble, Robert: 117

O'Brien, Margaret: 41
O'Faolain, Sean: 23, 113
Olvera, Judge: 75
Olvera Street: 75–76
O'Melveny, Henry: 109
Ord, Lieutenant E. O. C.: 104
Ortega family: 103f.
Otis, General Harrison Gray: 85, 88ff., 91–95, 108

Pacific Electric Railway: 27, 52
Palomares, Manuel: 79
Palomares, Don Ygnacio: 78
Palou, Father: 102
Parker, William H.: 52
Parsons, Louella: 41

Pereira, William: 60, 113
Petranilla, Feliz: 106
Pico, Andrés: 81
Pico, Pío: 56, 81
Pico House: 75
Pico Mansion: 81
Pirandello, Luigi: 27
Plantin Press: 66
Plaza Project: 64
Portola: 107
Port of Long Beach: 17
Port of Los Angeles: 14–17
Powdermaker, Hortense: 42
Powell, Lawrence Clark: 68
Preminger, Otto: 37f.
Publishers' Weekly: 66

Ramsaye, Terry: 40
Rancheros: 10, 57, 61, 74–75, 81, 83, 102, 105
Rancho Ex-Mission de San Fernando: 81
Rancho Guajome: 82–83
Rancho La Brea: 82
Rancho Los Alamitos: 80
Rancho Los Cerritos: 79–80
Rancho Los Feliz: 106
Rancho Los Palos Verdes: 82
Rancho San Juan Cajon de Santa Ana: 82
Rancho San Pascual: 107
Rancho Santa Anita: 76–77
Rand, Christopher: 123
RAND Corporation: 123
Reagan, Ronald: 86
Reid, Hugo: 77, 104
Reminiscences of a Ranger: 46
Ridge, John R.: 105–106
Ritchie, Ward: 66
Riverside Daily: 91
Rocha, Don Antonio: 82
Rodia, Simon: 64
Rogers, Roy: 40
Roosevelt, President Franklin Delano: 50
Rosecrans, General William S.: 16
Ross, A. W.: 29
Rosten, Leo C.: 41

Rubidoux, Carmelita: 79

Sanchez, Alcalde Vicente: 44
San Fernando Mission: 64, 81
San Francisco: 4–5
San Francisco *Chronicle*: 4
San Gorgonio Pass: 10, 11
San Pedro harbor: 14–17
Santa Fe Railway: 11
Santa Monica: 14–16
Saturday Evening Post, The: 4
Saturday Review: 37, 60
Savoy, Maggie: 97
Schindler, Rudolph M.: 66
Schulberg, Budd: 42, 43
Scott, Joseph: 94–95
Seidenbaum, Art: 97
Selig, Colonel William: 36
Shoshonean Indians: 10
Simpson, Sir George: 4
Sinclair, Upton: 117
Six Characters in Search of an Author: 27
Slide Area: Scenes of Hollywood Life, The: 41
Smith, Jack: 4–5, 97
Smith, Jedediah: 10–11
Southern California: 7
Southern California County: 50
Southern Pacific Railroad: 11, 14–15
Southwest Museum: 70, 82
Spider Boy: 42
Spring Street: 24–25
Stearns, Abel: 104
Stockton, Commodore Robert F.: 57
Stone, Irving: 110
Stroheim, Erich von: 41
Sullivan, Mrs. Senaida: 82
Swan, Howard: 57

Taft, President William H.: 110
Take the Witness: 15
Talmadge, Constance: 41
Talmadge, Norma: 41
Television: 37
Temple, Don Juan: 79–80

Thomas, Bob: 42
Time: 59
Times Building, bombing of: 92–94
Times Mirror Company: 89, 94
Tingley, Katharine: 116
Townsend, Dr. Francis: 117
Tuchman, Maurice: 112
Turnverein Hall: 57

Union Pacific System: 11

Valley Times: 87
Van Vechten, Carl: 42
Violence In the City: 51

Wagenknecht, Edward: 41
Wagner, Henry R.: 67
Wall Street Journal: 87, 95ff.
Warren, Earl: 50
Watts Riot: 51–53
Waugh, Evelyn: 120
Weinstock, Matt: 97
West, Mae: 41
West, Nathaniel: 43
Westways: 6

What Makes Sammy Run?: 43
What They Say About the Angels: 3
White, Senator Stephen M.: 14–15, 16
Wiggins, Frank: 115
Wilcox, Horace H.: 36
Wilde, Oscar: 69
Willard, Charles Dwight: 101
William Andrews Clark Memorial Library: 69
Williams, Nick B.: 88
Wilshire Boulevard: 29, 31
Wilson, Harry Leon: 42
Winter, Robert: 64
Wright, Frank Lloyd: 63ff.

Yang-na: 25, 44, 98
Yorty, Mayor Samuel W.: 38, 102, 122

Zamorano, Agustin V.: 67
Zamorano Eighty: 67
Zukor, Adolph: 41